Moodle Teaching Techniques

Creative Ways to Use Moodle for Constructing
Online Learning Solutions

William H. Rice IV

BIRMINGHAM - MUMBAI

Moodle Teaching Techniques

Creative Ways to Use Moodle for Constructing Online Learning Solutions

First published: September 2007

Production Reference: 1120907

Published by Packt Publishing Ltd.
32 Lincoln Road
Olton
Birmingham, B27 6PA, UK.

ISBN 978-1-847192-84-4

www.packtpub.com

Cover Image by Vinayak Chittar (vinayak.chittar@gmail.com)

Credits

Author

William H. Rice IV

Reviewers

Mark Bailye

Gurudutt Talgery

Derrin Kent

Senior Acquisition Editor

David Barnes

Development Editor

Rashmi Phadnis

Technical Editor

Sarvesh Shanbhag

Editorial Manager

Dipali Chittar

Project Manager

Patricia Weir

Project Coordinator

Sagara Naik

Indexer

Bhushan Pangaonkar

Proofreader

Damian Carvill

Cathy Cumborlidge

Production Coordinator

Shantanu Zagade

Cover Designer

Shantanu Zagade

About the Author

William Rice is a software training professional who lives, works, and plays in the New York City. His indoor hobbies include writing books and spending way too much time reading sites like slashdot and 43folders. His outdoor hobbies include orienteering, rock climbing, and edible wild plants (a book on that is coming someday).

William is fascinated by the relationship between technology and society; how we create our tools, and how our tools in turn shape us. He is married to an incredible woman who encourages his writing pursuits, and has two amazing sons.

He can be reached through his website at `http://www.williamrice.com`.

About the Reviewers

Gurudutt Talgery has wide-ranging industry experience in the areas of software development, software process, and product engineering with the Indian arms of reputed transnational technology companies. His current interests include content management, search applications, and information retrieval using open-source solution stacks.

Gurudutt finds a strong similarity between the spiritual freedom propounded by the ancient Indian Vedanta philosophy and the empowering freedom provided by the modern-day Open Source Software(OSS) movement. He single handedly manages a no-frills, multilingual India-centric search engine: www.bhramara.in. He can be reached via his blog at www.bhramara.in/blog.

Derrin Kent describes himself as a cross between a "teacher", a "geek", and an "HR/Project Manager". He is a founder, director, trainer, consultant, and a general dogsbody for The Development Manager Ltd. http://tdm.info. Derrin understands how e-learning and open-source software solutions can help workplace organisations to simultaneously improve both staff performance/satisfaction as well as the corporate bottom line. Derrin has been delivering work-based learning since 1992 and has supported a wide variety of workplace organisations with e-learning and open source including UK government bodies, large national charities, large national accrediting bodies, multi-site vocational training provider organisations, and networks of small local businesses.

Mark Bailye is currently working in the field of Medical Education where he has worked for ten years and has developed a great interest in learning and teaching. He has a proven track record in both online and face-to-face education and training. He is passionate about education and technology and wherever possible, incorporates the latest information and communication technologies into his teaching in order to enhance, engage and enrich the learner's experience.

I would also like thank PACKT Publishing and in particular Rashmi for giving me the opportunity to review this book.

For Gavin Bradford;
you showed us we really can
feel that way again. And for Lisa; you did it again!
Thanks for encouraging me and making this book possible.

Table of Contents

Preface

It's time for software manuals to evolve. I've been teaching software and writing manuals for about twenty years now, and have found that most software manuals are missing the most important information. While most of these do a good job of telling you how to perform tasks, that is, what buttons to push and menus to choose, they often leave the two most important questions unanswered:

- **What** effect will doing this have on your audience's experience?
- **When** would you want to do this?

For example, it would be nice if the manual that came with your word processor told you more than how to create tables and graphs. It would be even better if it also told you what kind of information is most easily understood in a table, as against a graph.

In this book, I hope to take a more evolved approach. I want to share techniques for creating effective learning solutions using Moodle, the world's most popular online learning management system. I'll give you keystroke-and-click directions to create these solutions. I'll also tell you what effect they'll have on your students' experience, and how to make best use of these solutions. You can let me know if I've succeeded (or not) by sending comments to us at feedback@packtpub.com, making sure that you have mentioned the book title in the subject of your message.

What is Moodle?

Moodle is a free, open-source Learning Management System (LMS). It is designed to help educators and trainers create online courses with opportunities for rich interaction with their students. It is the world's most popular online learning system. It will run on most low-cost hosting services, and probably on your company's or school's web server.

Moodle offers teachers and course designers a toolbox full of powerful, interactive online teaching tools. This book shows you how to use those tools to create effective learning solutions. These learning solutions are based on proven and accepted instructional principles, and traditional classroom activities, such as Distributed Practice, Self Monitoring, Pre-correction, and more. This book shows you how to creatively use Moodle's online learning features in ways that adhere to proven educational principles.

What This Book Covers

Chapter 1: Introduction, expalins the approach the book will take for creating learning solutions, and briefly describes the educational principles and practices upon which the techniques are based.

Chapter 2: Forum Solutions, offers you solutions for managing your forums. The first two sections focus on making the best use of forums. The last two sections of this chapter, focus on managing your forums.

Chapter 3: Chat Solutions, gives you a key to making the best use of Moodle's — or any LMS's — chat function, in a way that takes advantage of its unique strengths, instead of trying to make it act like a face-to-face meeting. In this chapter, we explore the questions "What is chat good for?" and "How can I achieve success in an online chat?" Considering the fact that Moodle's chat functions are similar to most other chat software, the answers to these questions apply to more than just Moodle.

Chapter 4: Quiz Solutions, tells you that a quiz can be more than just a test. At its best, a quiz can also become a learning experience. Moodle offers features that help you to accomplish that. This chapter gives you five ways to use Moodle quizzes for more than testing.

Chapter 5: Lesson Solutions, tells you that a Moodle lesson can be a powerful combination of instruction and assessment. Lessons offer the flexibility of a web page, the interactivity of a quiz, and branching capabilities.

Chapter 6: Wiki Solutions, tells you that a wiki is a powerful tool for collaboration, and it does enable students to participate in a group activity from anywhere at any time. However, a wiki can also be a powerful tool for individualized learning. This principle is called "differential learning", which means that the learning experience should be customized for each student, depending on his/her learning ability. With individual wikis, you can differentiate the learning experience for your students.

Chapter 7: Glossary Solutions, tells you that glossaries are not just special-purpose, online dictionaries, but can also be an enjoyable, collaborative activity for your class, and a teaching tool.

Chapter 8: The Choice Activity, tells you that a choice activity is the simplest type of activities. You can use a choice to: take a quick poll, ask students to choose sides in a debate, confirm the students' understanding of an agreement, and gather consent.

Chapter 9: Course Solution, focuses on making your course easier to navigate. The goal of all these solutions is to reduce the time and effort your students spend in figuring out what to do next, so they can get on with the learning. Sometimes, just slightly reducing the effort that students make on navigating through your course, requires a great effort on your part. But, anything you do to help your students navigate easily through your course is worth the effort. The result is less time spent wondering what to do next, and more time spent on the course content.

Chapter 10: Workshop Solution, tells you that it is one of the most complex and powerful, of activities. This chapter takes you through the process of creating a full-featured workshop. It focuses on helping you to make decisions that create the kind of workshop experience you want for your students.

Who is this book for?

The book is written for educators, corporate trainers, university professors, and others who have a basic knowledge of Moodle. If you don't know how to create basic courseware in Moodle, you can still use this book. But, you will need to learn those basics as you build the solutions in this book. You can use the online help, the forums on moodle.org, a basic Moodle book, and trial-and-error to fill in the gap in your knowledge.

Conventions

In this book, you will find a number of styles of text that distinguish between different kinds of information. Here are some examples of these styles, and an explanation of their meaning.

There are three styles for code. Code words in text are shown as follows: "The file `Microscopy.txt` will have links to the other three pages. In the Wiki Markup language, links are encased in square brackets, like this: `[The_Light_Microscope]`".

A block of code will be set as follows:

```
!!!Microscopy and Specimen Preparation
[Lenses and the Bending of Light | Lenses_and_the_Bending_of_
Light]
[The Light Microscope |The_Light_Microscope]
[Preparation and Staining of Specimens | Preparation_and_Staining_
of_Specimens]
```

New terms and **important words** are introduced in a bold-type font.

Words that you see on the screen, in menus or dialog boxes for example, appear in our text like this: "From the **Add an activity...** drop-down list, select **Forum**, as shown in the following screenshot".

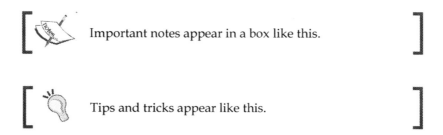

Important notes appear in a box like this.

Tips and tricks appear like this.

Reader Feedback

Feedback from our readers is always welcome. Let us know what you think about this book, what you liked or disliked. Reader feedback is important for us to develop titles that you get the most out of.

To send us general feedback, simply drop an email to feedback@packtpub.com, making sure to mention the book title in the subject of your message.

If there is a book that you need and would like to see us publish, please send us a note in the **SUGGEST A TITLE** form on www.packtpub.com or email suggest@packtpub.com.

If there is a topic that you have expertise in and you are interested in either writing or contributing to a book, see our author guide on www.packtpub.com/authors.

Customer Support

Now that you are the proud owner of a Packt book, we have a number of things to help you to get the most from your purchase.

Downloading the Example Code for the Book

Visit `http://www.packtpub.com/support`, and select this book from the list of titles, to download any example code or extra resources for this book. The files available for download will then be displayed.

The downloadable files contain instructions on how to use them.

Errata

Although we have taken every care to ensure the accuracy of our contents, mistakes do happen. If you find a mistake in one of our books — maybe a mistake in text or code — we would be grateful if you would report this to us. By doing this you can save other readers from frustration, and help to improve subsequent versions of this book. If you find any errata, report them by visiting `http://www.packtpub.com/support`, selecting your book, clicking on the **Submit Errata** link, and entering the details of your errata. Once your errata are verified, your submission will be accepted and the errata are added to the list of existing errata. The existing errata can be viewed by selecting your title from `http://www.packtpub.com/support`.

Questions

You can contact us at `questions@packtpub.com` if you are having a problem with some aspect of the book, and we will do our best to address it.

1
Introduction

Welcome to *Moodle Teaching Techniques*! Moodle offers teachers and course designers a toolbox full of online teaching tools. This book shows you how to use those tools to create effective learning solutions. These learning solutions are based on proven, accepted instructional principles, and traditional classroom activities.

Moodle is a **Course Management System** (**CMS**) for producing web-based courses. It is a **Free Open Source Software** (**FOSS**), which means that you are free to use, modify, and redistribute it as long as you:

- Provide the source to others
- Do not modify or remove the original license and copyrights
- Apply this same license to any derivative work

Under these conditions, thousands of developers have contributed features and functionality to Moodle. The result is the world's most popular, free, and feature-packed online learning system.

The Moodle Advantage

Many of the features in Moodle, are carefully chosen to support a philosophy of learning, called "social constructionist pedagogy". Simply stated, this style of learning and teaching is based upon four concepts:

1. Students acquire new knowledge as they interact with their environment, your course activities, and other students.

2. Students learn more when they construct learning experiences for others. You might be familiar with the "learning pyramid" which states that students remember 10% of what they read, 20% of what they hear, 30% of what is demonstrated to them, 50% of what they discuss, and 75% of what they practice. That same pyramid states that students retain 90% of what they teach others. You can check the learning pyramid at:

    `http://homepages.gold.ac.uk/polovina/learnpyramid/about.html`

3. When students become part of a culture, they are constantly learning. For example, you and your partner would probably learn more about ballroom dancing when you're in a dance class, versus watching a video together. The interaction with other students and possibly a variety of teachers would enrich and accelerate your learning process.

4. Some students try to remain objective and factual, some try to accept more subjective views, and others try to integrate both approaches. Constructed behavior is when a student can choose whichever approach is more appropriate.

You are probably not accustomed to an application's features being chosen based upon a philosophy. Usually, features are chosen based only on what is technically feasible and what customers are willing to pay for. These certainly are factors for the Moodle developers. However, the educational philosophy behind Moodle is also a criterion for adding features. This gives Moodle a tremendous advantage.

As Moodle is designed around a well-defined educational philosophy, its user interface is very consistent. I don't just mean in the traditional sense, where you compare the icons, colors, menu actions, and layout on each page to ensure they match. As you go through a Moodle site, things look, feel, and function consistently. But more importantly, you interact with each activity, your classmates, and the teacher in a consistent way, whether it's in the chat room, a forum, or leaving feedback on a workshop. When interaction becomes easier, the student can focus more on learning, and less on the software.

What will We Accomplish with this Book?

When a teacher begins using an online learning system, the first thing most of us do is explore the system's features. We discover it has online forums, electronic flashcards, interactive quizzes, Wikis, collaborative workshops, and other features. Our question now becomes, "How can I use this feature to teach my course?" or "What features of this software can be used to effectively teach my course?". For example, we discover the software has an `Assignment` module and ask, "How can

I use online assignments in my course?". We start by exploring the software and asking how we can use it to effectively teach our courses. When given a new tool, it's natural to explore the tool's functions and think of ways to use it.

This book gives you solutions that help you make the most of the many features found in a standard Moodle installation. Some of these solutions require several hours to build. Others are just a matter of selecting a single option in one of Moodle's setup pages.

Effective learning and teaching principles are not just for academic teachers. If you're a corporate trainer, your students will benefit from the learning solutions in this book. These solutions are based on instructional practices that have been proven to work for young and adult learners.

I'll give you enough step-by-step instruction to create each solution in Moodle, and information about each solution to understand its basic theory. This understanding will enable you to determine if that practice will work for your students in your course. For example, I'll discuss the role of immediate feedback in the learning process. Then, I'll describe how to use immediate feedback when you administer a quiz. You must decide if immediate feedback is appropriate for your class and learning objectives. If you decide that it is, I'll show you how to enable feedback for each type of quiz question, and for the quiz as a whole.

In the chapter on Lessons, we'll discuss the role of sequential versus non-sequential activities in a class. I'll show you how to use a lesson to structure learning material so that the student must proceed in a given sequence. Then, we'll discuss some creative uses of Lessons: as an alternative to Quizzes, a flash card deck, and to review step-by-step instructions for an assigned activity.

Some Moodle Requisites

You don't need to be an expert Moodle teacher, or course creator to use the solutions in this book. However, this book assumes that you can use Moodle's basic features. You can learn Moodle before reading this book, or learn it as you practice implementing these solutions.

For example, one of the learning solutions in this book is "Guided Notes". This solution uses Moodle's standard wiki module. To implement the solution, you need to know how to create a wiki in Moodle. You could learn how to create a wiki from another book on basic Moodle usage, from the online help, or from the moodle.org forums. However, this book will not give step-by-step directions for creating the wiki. It will give directions for adapting the wiki for Guided Notes.

If you're new to Moodle, consider practicing on the Moodle demonstration Site at `http://demo.moodle.org/`.

Standard Modules

Moodle is an open-source software, so new modules are constantly being developed and contributed by the Moodle community. The modules that are a part of Moodle's core distribution are covered in this book. Moodle's capabilities are enhanced by additional modules, which enable better learning solutions.

Some of the techniques in this book are workarounds that could be directly accomplished by adding a third-party module to your Moodle site. However, as each new version of Moodle is released, only the standard modules are guaranteed compatible. There is no guarantee that a third-party module, which you have installed will be compatible with future versions of Moodle. This can hold back the upgrade process for your site.

All of the solutions in this book can be implemented with Moodle's standard modules. I encourage you to explore the add-on modules available on the site `www.moodle.org`.

Instructional Principles and Activities

The solutions in this book are based on accepted, research-based instructional principles and traditional learning activities. Learning principles can be applied to a wide variety of activities. For example, the principles of Distributed Practice and Immediate Error Correction can be applied to `Quiz`, `Lesson`, and `Assignment` activities in Moodle. When we step through the solutions for quizzes, lessons, and assignments, I'll briefly discuss how to apply these learning principles to those activities.

Examples of traditional learning activities are: timed quizzes, flash cards, and Socratic questioning. These activities have a long history of success in the classroom. I'll show you how to implement them online.

If you're interested in learning more about these principles and activities, each is described in a subsection later in this chapter. If you'd rather proceed directly to the solutions, you can safely skip this section. You don't need a background in learning theory to use this book. However, a brief introduction to these instructional principles and traditional activities will tell you why the techniques in this book work, and also might stimulate further ideas of your own.

Big Ideas

The balanced nature of an equation is an example of a big idea in algebra. *Supply and demand* is an example of a big idea in economics. These big ideas help students see the common themes in diverse facts.

The examples of sources for the big ideas are as follows:

- **Corporate Objectives**: Improving the customer experience for our call center can be one of your company's corporate objectives. You could break that down into a skill set to be taught using Moodle, such as, *Product Knowledge*, *Handling Objections*, and *Building a Customer Relationship*. While teaching each of these skills, you would constantly refer back to the big idea of improving the customer experience.

- **Educational standards**: The state can mandate that the relationship of technology to society be part of a social studies curriculum.

- **Established research:** For example, the Big Bang is a generally-accepted big idea in science.

- **The teacher's knowledge of the central themes in the subject**: A photography teacher may have deep understanding of the effect that depth of field has on photographic composition, and make this one of the big ideas in the course.

Knowing many disconnected facts is not enough for developing expertise. Big ideas enable students to make meaningful generalizations about the facts they learn. They give students a framework into which they can put new knowledge. A big idea can help the student determine where a piece of information fits into the big picture, and how that information relates to what (s)he already knows.

Experts structure their knowledge around the big ideas of their disciplines. Experts' strategies for thinking and solving problems are linked to their understanding of big ideas. Understanding the big ideas also allows experts to see the similarities between new problems and those previously encountered.

Several solutions in this book help you to implement big ideas in your courses. You will see how a wiki and a static HTML block can be used to bring big ideas online.

Distributed Practice

Distributed practice is when a student studies and practices during many sessions that are short in length. These sessions are distributed over a long time period. This is the opposite of cramming. Distributed practice sessions are short and usually intense.

Distributed practice allows time between learning sessions for knowledge to become permanent. Research shows that "sleeping on it" actually helps us to sort through new information, and make permanent the most important new information (see `http://www.seedmagazine.com/news/2006/07/how_we_know.php`).

Distributing practice across different days, instead of having the practice sessions all on the same day, greatly improves students' retention (Refer to: Distributed practice in verbal recall tasks: A review and quantitative synthesis by Nicholas et. al.). With the right settings, Moodle's `Quiz` module can be used to distributed practice quizzes across any time period.

Guided Notes

Guided Notes are notes provided by the teacher to the student with an outline for a presentation or reading. The outline contains labels for the main points and supporting details of the material. As the teacher or reading material elaborates on each point of the outline, the student fills in the details.

Research shows that when students are given an outline for taking notes in class, they do better on test questions that are complex, or that require analytical skills. Also, most students prefer the guided note taking approach to taking their own notes. For more in-depth information, see *Effects of Guided Notes Versus Completed Notes during Lectures on College Students' Quiz Performance* at `http://www.pubmedcentral.nih.gov/articlerender.fcgi?artid=1389604`.

This book will show you how to implement guided notes using an individual student wiki, with pre-made starting pages.

Immediate Error Correction

Immediate error correction improves the accuracy and speed with which a student can recall knowledge. It requires correcting a student as soon as the student makes an error, and immediately providing the correct response. Immediate correction reduces the number of times a student must repeat information before learning it.

In a face-to-face class, if a student gives an incorrect answer, you might verbally correct the student, and then ask the student to repeat the correct information. If the student gives a correct answer, you might acknowledge the correct response and then refer back to the prior information to build connections in the student's knowledge. For example, you might say, "Yes! Remember, we discussed this issue at the very beginning of the chapter when we were talking about…"

In an online course, you must program the system to respond to correct and incorrect answers. I'll show you how to use Moodle's `Quiz` and `Lesson` modules to implement immediate error correction.

Juxtapose Examples and Non-Examples

To juxtapose items, is to place them side-by-side, or to present them in a rapid alternating sequence. Juxtaposing examples and non-examples of a concept, rule, or strategy can be effective when you are introducing new material.

Examples help the student to discover what the items have in common. This helps the student to form generalizations. Non-examples help the student to discover how the items differ from the rest of the world. This helps the student to recognize and differentiate the concept, rule, or strategy being taught. Generalizing and differentiating enables the student to make independent use of the concept, rule, or strategy.

For example, if you are teaching about mammals, you might present the following examples and non-examples:

Examples	Non-examples
Cat	Lizard
Dolphin	Shark
Bat	Robin
Badger	Platypus

When placing examples and non-examples in a sequence, group them according to the similarity or difference of their attributes. In the table above, you can see that I grouped four-legged land animals (cat and lizard), sea creatures (dolphin and shark), and flying creatures (bat and robin).

You should also vary the items to include:

- Examples that are obvious, such as **cat** in the table above.
- Examples that are less obvious, such as **bat** in the table above.
- Non-examples that are almost but not quite, such as **platypus** in the table above.

Immediately after presenting a sequence of examples and non-examples in a face-to-face class, you might ask the student to create new examples and non-examples. You would provide immediate feedback to the student about the examples/non-examples.

In an online class, you can accomplish something similar:

1. Offer a series of examples/non-examples.

2. Immediately after viewing the series, the student takes an online quiz during which (s)he identifies items as examples and non-examples. The quiz gives immediate feedback for correct and incorrect answers.

3. Assign the student the task of generating his/her own list of examples and non-examples. Specify a due date in the near future, and grade the assignments promptly.

Moodle's `Lesson` module is a good tool for rapidly presenting examples and non-examples. I'll show you how to use a lesson to create an online flash card deck.

Lesson Outline

A lesson outline gives your student a preview of what is to come. This preview is proven to help learners remember and integrate content. A lesson outline serves as a visual map that enables students to see what they've learned and what they will learn. Looking back at prior knowledge helps students to integrate it with the new knowledge that they are learning. Also, a visual organizer helps students to stay motivated because they can see their progress through the class.

Moodle's topics and labels provide an easy way to give your students an effective lesson outline.

Mnemonics and Other Reminders

As teachers and trainers, we get more satisfaction from teaching concepts, skills, and analytical thinking than we do from making our students memorize facts. However, some subjects simply require students to memorize things. To make memorization less tedious for our students, we can use mnemonics and reminders. First-letter mnemonics, peg-words, and keywords are all examples of this technique.

Moodle's glossary feature can be used to hold reminders and mnemonics. Quiz feedback can also be used to give the student reminders. This book will show you how to apply those solutions in your courses.

Pre-Correction

Effective pre-correction is one of the signs that tell us that a teacher has mastered both the material being taught, and the ability to teach that material.

The teacher uses clear instructions when anticipating errors that students might make before the students have an opportunity to make those errors. Pre-correction is helpful when the majority of a class requires repeated directions, remediation, or reminders to stay engaged during a lesson.

Sometimes, the need for pre-correction becomes apparent only after the teacher has taught the material. Other times, an experienced teacher can predict when pre-correction will be needed even before teaching the material.

A Google search for the phrase *pre-correction instructional strategy* shows that most research into pre-correction focuses on using it as a classroom control strategy, to reduce behavioral problems. In a traditional classroom, we use pre-correction to state the rules for interaction among the students. In an online course, when we help novice online learners to understand the rules of online interaction, we are using pre-correction.

Pre-correction can be used to:

- Tell students where and when to begin: Start with the first reading under Topic 2. Do not skip this reading.
- Emphasize a rule: Workshop assessments must state which criteria you are using as the basis of your comment.
- Restate newly-acquired knowledge that will be used in the upcoming activity: Before attempting the quiz, refresh your memory of the formulas for cosine, sine, and tangent.
- Anticipate problems and challenges that new online learners might have: At least one full day before our scheduled chat session, try to access the Open Chat area of the course. If your browser can run the chat software, you should see...

Workshops, lessons, and topic zero are all Moodle features that can be used to implement pre-correction online.

Response Cards

Response cards provide the students with opportunities for active and frequent responses. In a traditional classroom, the teacher poses a question to the entire class. The students answer by holding up a card that has their answer on it. Response cards can be pre-printed with frequent responses, such as "yes" and "no". Or, they can be blank for students to write their own responses. The teacher must use a signal so that students know when to hold up their response cards. Online, the teacher must also use a signal to let students know when to respond.

Don't confuse response cards with a one-question quiz. The table lists some of the differences between a quiz and response cards:.

Quiz	Response Cards
Grading and correction is usually done by the software.	Teacher usually scans all of the students' responses and provides correction on-the-spot.
Usually done by each student individually.	Usually done by the entire class, at the same time.
Students don't see each other's responses until after the quiz is graded, if at all.	Students see each other's responses when they happen.
Usually used to test competence, for a grade.	Usually used to build competence, and is ungraded.

The differences between a quiz and response cards, using an online quiz to create the experience of response cards probably won't work well so we'll need to use a different tool.

Response cards are especially useful when you want to create a fast-paced instructional environment. Consider using them to build competence in subjects where students will need to recall knowledge quickly, such as a foreign language.

You can also use response cards to judge a class's progress. A few questions in the middle of a lesson can tell you if you need to make any mid-course corrections to the class.

You can also use response cards to get feedback from the class. In an online environment, you don't have the benefit of seeing the students' faces to determine if they're confused, frustrated, or bored. If you need to determine a class's mood, or suspect that you are "losing them", consider using response cards to gather feedback about their thoughts and feelings toward the course.

Choices and chats are two Moodle features that can be used to implement response card learning online.

Self-Monitoring

Self-monitoring is when a student checks his or her knowledge against an established standard. In a traditional class, a student might solve homework problems and compare his or her answers to those given at the back of the book. In an online class, you can use Moodle's quiz module to create and track quizzes for self-monitoring. I'll show you how to make quizzes ungraded, and how to reveal and hide them at appropriate times during the course. The physical placement of these self-tests in a course can also be an important part of implementing self-monitoring.

Socratic Dialogue

Socratic dialog is a *discussion* between the teacher and students. The teacher uses questions to probe the student's knowledge, and to require the student to use rules of reasoning. That is, the teacher uses questions designed to elicit prior knowledge, and to lead the student to discover new knowledge. Socratic dialogue requires the student and teacher to focus on the discussion, and to actively engage with each other.

You may have seen research stating that students remember only about 10% of what they read, and about 50% of what they discuss. A Socratic dialogue for each topic can be an effective review session, and help the student to retain more material. It also gives the teacher a chance to determine how well the students are learning the material.

Socratic dialogue requires one-to-one communication between the student and teacher. I'll show you how to use forums and wikis in a focused way, to achieve a Socratic dialogue between you and your students.

Time Trials

Time trials are a quick and fun method for a student to solidify a skill which (s)he has recently mastered. This practice helps the student to develop confidence and fluidity with a new skill. When used to develop knowledge, instead of as a graded test, a time trial should always have more problems than the student can complete. In a traditional classroom, time trials are usually one minute or less. They are used at least once daily, sometimes more often. Time trials offer an opportunity for short, intense practice sessions.

One of the main purposes of a time trial is building the student's confidence. Presenting time trials in a stressful, threatening way can defeat this purpose. Also, making a time trial too long can make it stressful. In most cases, you want a time trial to be stressful enough to engage the student, but not so stressful that you risk damaging the student's confidence with an activity that is too difficult. A notable exception to this is when you are testing knowledge or skills that must be used under stress. For example, suppose you are testing an emergency room nurse's knowledge of a procedure. You could use several quick, relatively easy time trials to build the nurse's confidence. Then follow those with a final, extended, and comprehensive time trial to test the nurse under stress.

Time trials should be used only to practice a skill in which a student is competent. This practice is an effective finishing technique, but not a very useful technique for teaching new information. Use a time trial after a student has been taught the material, and has successfully completed an untimed test of the material. The untimed test builds the student's confidence enough to attempt the timed test. The timed test builds the student's confidence enough to apply the material to real-world situations.

A time trial can also be used at the beginning of a lesson, to reveal the limits of a student's competence. So in addition to solidifying knowledge, a time trial can demonstrate to the student what (s)he doesn't know. For example, at the beginning of a semester you can give a science class three minutes to classify a list of astronomical objects. Ask them to classify each object as a planet, moon, comet, star, galaxy, nebula, or other body. The result of this exercise would make the student aware of his/her knowledge or lack of knowledge of astronomy. A similar time trial at the end of the unit would demonstrate how much the student has learned. Allow students to see their own grades, and post the class's average grade as well. Repeat the time trial at the end of the course. Now the students can compare their grades at the beginning and end of the course.

Moodle's quiz module can be used to deliver timed trials.

Instructional Principles and Activities Mapped to Moodle Features

The following table maps each of the instructional principles and classroom activities discussed in the previous sections, to a Moodle feature where we can implement that principle or activity:

Instructional Principle and Activity	Moodle Feature
Big Ideas	Forum
Distributed Practice	Quiz
Error Correction	Assignment Lesson Logs Quiz
Example/Non-example	Lesson
Guided Notes	Wiki
Lesson Outline	Topics and Courses

Instructional Principle and Activity	Moodle Feature
Mnemonics and Reminders	Glossary Quiz
Pre-Correction	Lesson Workshop
Response Cards	Choice
Self-Monitoring	Quiz
Socratic Dialogue	Forums

Summary

This chapter presented various teaching methods such as big ideas, distributed practice, guided notes, etc., which help the teacher or trainer in putting the ideas across to the students in an effective manner. It also explained various activities, which aid teaching such as conducting quizzes, use of response cards, time trials and so on, to make learning an enjoyable and a gainful experience.

2
Forum Solutions

Forums are one of Moodle's most powerful features. A well-run class forum can stimulate a thoughtful discussion, motivate students to become involved, and provoke unexpected insights. However, a forum that has gone off track or gotten out of hand can stifle discussion, keep students away from the class, and degrade into irrelevant discussion. This chapter offers you solutions for managing your forums. The first two sections in this chapter focus on making the best use of forums. The last two sections focus on managing your forums.

Single-Student Forum

A student always focusses better when (s)he gets personalized attention from the teacher. The exchange can be unplanned, such as when a teacher answers the student's question in class. Or it can be planned, such as when a teacher uses the Socratic dialogue method to guide a conversation with the student (see *Socratic Dialogue* in *Chapter 1: Introduction*). Whatever form it takes, individual attention and active dialogue with the teacher, inspires most students to focus.

In an online course, you can give students individual attention by creating a private forum for each student. Only you and the student can access that student's forum. This creates a private conversation space with several advantages.

If the student knows that other students will not see the forum, (s)he won't worry about asking "stupid questions" in front of class. In both school and the corporate world, the kinds of questions that students are most embarrassed to ask are exactly the kinds of questions that most need to be answered. These "stupid questions" often deal with background information and assumptions that are very basic, and necessary to understanding the topic being studied.

With only two participants the student will find it much easier to find and follow the history of your conversation. The continuity won't be lost among other students' postings. You will find it easier to guide a conversation between yourself and just one student, than a conversation among the entire class. You now have a threaded discussion between student and teacher, showing the history and progress of the discussion.

Why not a Single-Student Wiki Instead?

In *Chapter 6: Wiki Solutions*, we discuss using a single-student wiki. That would also work for giving the student individual attention, and creating a single-student wiki for each student in your class is much easier and faster than creating a forum for each student. Creating the individual wikis can be done with a simple setting.

However, a single-student wiki works best when the author uses it to speak to a group, and to get feedback from his or her readers. A forum is designed to support active conversation, and to keep a history of that conversation. So while a wiki makes a good tool for collaborating on a project, a forum is the better tool for conversing about a topic. If the result of the discussion is most important, consider a single-student wiki; it makes collaboration easier. If the discussion itself is most important, consider the extra effort of creating many single-student forums, since they display the thread and history.

Creating Single-Student Forums

As of this writing, Moodle (version 1.9) does not support the creation of individual student forums. However, Moodle does enable you to create a separate forum for each group in a class. We can use the groups feature as a workaround, and create the effect of many single-student forums. We do this by creating a group for each student in our class, and then creating a forum with the groups feature activated.

Create a Forum for Each Student/Group

When creating the course, add a forum that will segregate each group. That is, each group will have their own forum. You can allow each group to see the other groups' forums, but they will not be allowed to edit other groups' forums. Or, you can make each groups' forum invisible to the others.

Remember that each group will consist of only a single student. So in this process, when we discuss groups, we're really talking about individual students.

The following steps illustrate how to create a separate forum for each group in your course:

1. From the **Add an activity…** drop-down list, select **Forum**, as shown in the following screenshot:

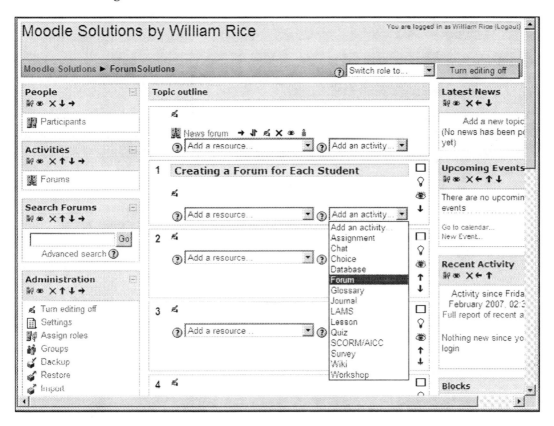

2. Enter a **name** and **type** for the forum. In the following example, I'm using **A single simple discussion** to create a single-topic forum, where all the postings will be displayed on the same page. This makes the history of the student-teacher discussion very easy to see. That type of forum is most useful for short, focused discussions.

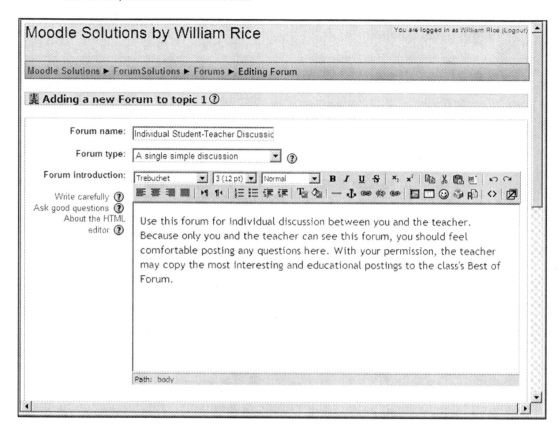

3. By selecting **Yes, forever** for **Force everyone to be subscribed?** in the following screenshot, you ensure that all students are subscribed automatically, even students that enroll at a later time.

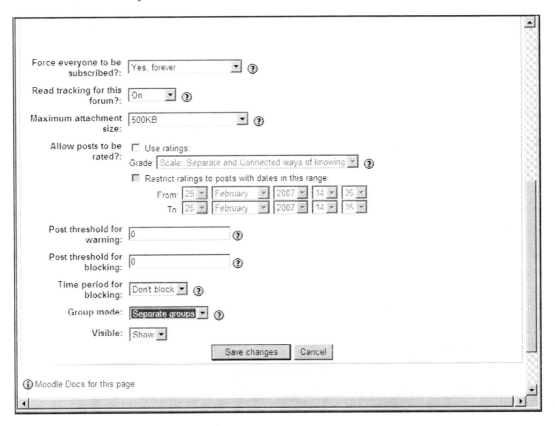

4. The key setting here is **Group mode**. When we select **Separate groups**, we create a separate forum for each group in the class. In the next section, we will create a group for each student. The result is a separate forum for each student, available only to that student and the teacher, where they can hold private conversation.

5. Save the forum settings and continue.

Enrolling Students

If you have not already enrolled students in the course, you should do so before creating the groups. If the students are already enrolled, skip to *Create a Group for Each Student* in the next section.

The following steps illustrate how to enroll students, manually in your course:

1. Open the course into which you want to enrol the students. Then, from the **Administration** drop-down box, select **Assign roles**.

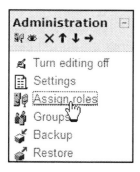

2. On the **Assign roles** page, as shown below, select **Student**.

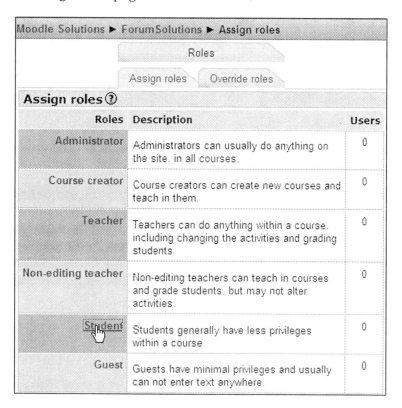

3. Ensure the **Role to assign** drop-down list is set to **Student**. Then, from the list of potential users on the right, select one user. Click the left-facing arrow to enrol that user in your course. Refer to the following screenshot:

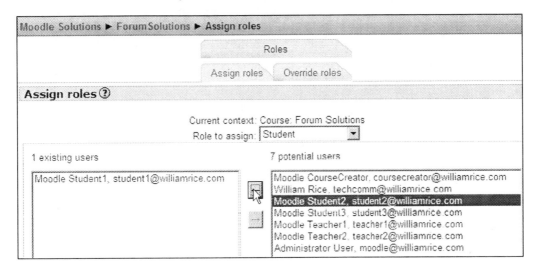

Repeat this for each student. If you want to remove a student from the course, select the student from the list on the left, and click the right-facing arrow.

6. To exit this page, select the course name from the navigation breadcrumbs at the top of the page. This will put you back into your course's home page, and then you can continue with creating a group for each student.

Create a Group for Each Student

After all of your students are enrolled, go into the course and create a group for each student.

The following steps illustrate how to create groups and assign students to them:

1. From the **Administration** block, shown as follows, select **Groups**.

2. From the **Current role** drop-down list as shown in the following screenshot, select **Student**. This ensures that you are seeing only users who are enrolled as students in this course. Then, in the field above the **Add new group** button, enter the name of the first group. Name the group after the student for whom you created it. In this example, I created a group for Moodle Student1 called Student1, and I am about to create a group for Moodle Student2 called Student2.

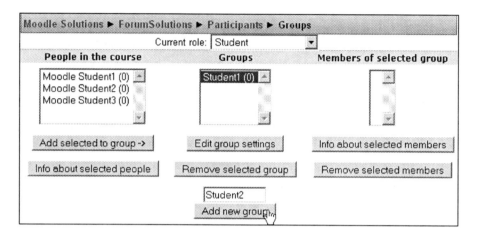

3. After creating all of the groups, add one student to each group. In the following example, you can see that the group **Student1** is selected, and **Moodle Student1** is a member of that group.

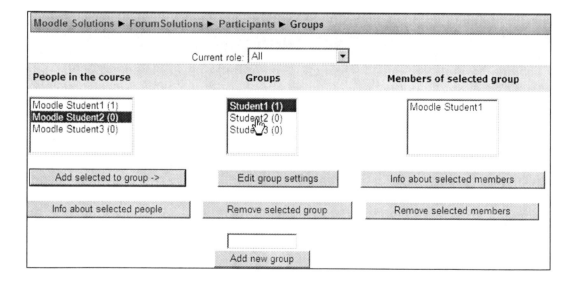

To assign a student to a group:
- ° Select the group. In the preceding example, you can see the user is about to select the group **Student2**.
- ° Select the student to add to the group.
- ° Click the **Add selected to group** button.
- ° Repeat as needed.

4. To exit this page, select the course name from the navigation breadcrumbs at the top of the page. This will put you back into your course's home page.

The student's private forum will look like any other Moodle forum. However, only the student and teacher will have access to it.

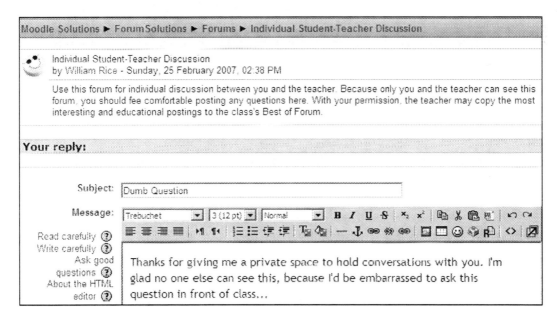

Motivate Students to Interact with a "Best-of" Forum

Getting students to participate in forums, chats, assessments, and other social activities online can be a challenge. Without the force of personality that comes from face-to-face contact, some students will not be motivated to participate. A best-of forum can provide additional motivation for students to participate in class activities. A best-of forum is a showcase for the best and most interesting student contributions to your class. As the teacher, you can copy students' contributions to wikis, forums, chats, assignments, and workshops, and post them in the forum. The possibility of having their "15 minutes of fame" can motivate some students to participate at a higher level.

Asking Permission and Setting a Policy

Some activities in Moodle are almost always individual. When students complete these activities, they have a reasonable expectation that their work will not be shared with the class. For example, when a student answers a quiz question, (s)he reasonably expects that what (s)he wrote will not be shared with the entire class. Other activities do not carry this expectation of privacy. For example, when a student posts to a forum, (s)he expects that posting to be read by the rest of the class.

Before posting work from a student in the best-of forum, consider if the student can reasonably expect that work to be private. If so, ask the student's permission before posting it. If the student is reluctant to have you post his or her work, you might want to anonymize the work. That is, remove anything from the work that would indicate which student created it. This might make the student more comfortable with having the work posted in the best-of forum.

If you expect to use a best-of forum in a class, you should clearly indicate that in the course syllabus and introduction. Don't make it a surprise. For some students, sharing their work in a public forum might be only a little less scary than public speaking. Inform the students ahead of time, and state your policy on how much information you will reveal about each student.

Which Type of Forum?

In Moodle, you can create several types of forums. Each type can be used in a different way for a best-of forum. The types of forums are:

Type of Forum	Description
Single simple discussion	The entire forum appears on one page. The first posting, at the top of the page, is the topic for the forum. This topic is usually created by the teacher. The students then post replies under this topic. A single-topic forum is most useful for short, highly-focused discussions.
Standard	In a standard forum, anyone can start a new topic. Teachers and students can create new topics and reply to existing postings.
Each person posts one discussion	Each student can create one and only one new topic. Everyone can reply to every topic.

Type of Forum	Description
Q and A	This is like a single-topic forum, in that the teacher creates the topic for the forum. Students then reply to that topic. However, a student cannot see anyone else's reply until (s)he has posted a reply. The topic is usually a question posed by the teacher, and the students' replies are usually answers to that question.

Each of these forum types can be used to create a different kind of best-of forum. The subsections coming up, cover the use of each forum type.

You select the forum type while creating the forum, on the **Editing Forum** page:

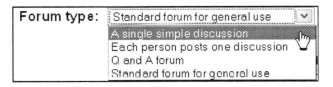

Single Simple Discussion Forum

The next screenshot is an example of a single-topic forum. The forum consists of one topic at the top of the page, and everything else on that page is a reply from the students. Readers can reply to the topic, but not create new ones.

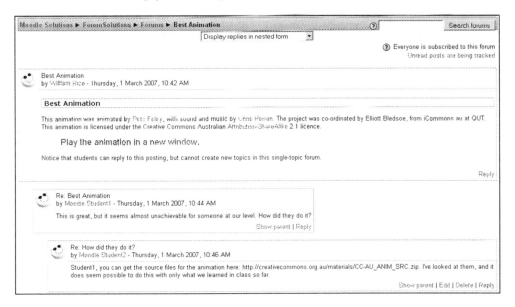

This is especially useful if you want to select the best work as an example for each topic or week in your course. You can always end each topic or week with the best work as an example so that, discussion can take place on it.

Standard Forum

In a standard forum, the default setting allows students to create new topics and post replies to the topics. This makes it an open forum, which would be useful, if you want your students to be able to post their own or someone else's best work. Following is an example of a multi-topic forum. Each piece of work is a new topic.

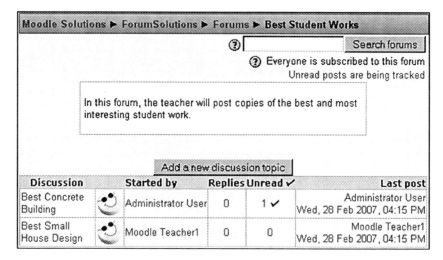

One way to keep the best-of forum organized is to allow only the teacher to create new topics. Each topic is an example of student work, posted by the teacher. Students discuss each example by replying to the topic. To accomplish this, you'll need to disable the students' ability to create new topics.

By default, the Student role in Moodle enables students to create new topics in a standard forum. You can disable this by referring to the following steps:

1. Select the forum in which you want to disable the students' ability to create new topics.

2. Select **Update this Forum**.

3. Select the **Roles** tab, and then the **Override roles** sub-tab, as shown in the following screenshot:

Roles	Description	Overrides
Administrator	Administrators can usually do anything on the site, in all courses.	0
Course creator	Course creators can create new courses and teach in them.	0
Teacher	Teachers can do anything within a course, including changing the activities and grading students.	0
Non-editing teacher	Non-editing teachers can teach in courses and grade students, but may not alter activities	2
Student	Students generally have less privileges within a course.	4
Guest	Guests have minimal privileges and usually can not enter text anywhere.	0

4. Select **Student**. This brings up the **Overrides** page.

Overrides ②

Current context: Activity module: A Standard forum for general use
Role to override: Student ▾

Capability	Inherit	Allow	Prevent	Prohibit	Risks
Core system					
Access all groups moodle/site:accessallgroups	⊙	○	○	○	
Forum					
View discussions mod/forum:viewdiscussion	⊙	○	○	○	
View hidden timed posts mod/forum:viewhiddentimedposts	⊙	○	○	○	
Start new discussions mod/forum:startdiscussion	○	⊙	○	○	S
Reply to posts mod/forum:replypost	○	⊙	○	○	S
View ratings mod/forum:viewrating	⊙	○	○	○	
View any ratings mod/forum:viewanyrating	○	⊙	○	○	
Rate posts mod/forum:rate	○	⊙	○	○	
Create attachments mod/forum:createattachment	⊙	○	○	○	S
Delete own posts (within deadline) mod/forum:deleteownpost	⊙	○	○	○	
Delete any posts (anytime) mod/forum:deleteanypost	⊙	○	○	○	
Split discussions mod/forum:splitdiscussions	⊙	○	○	○	
Move discussions mod/forum:movediscussions	⊙	○	○	○	
Edit any post mod/forum:editanypost	⊙	○	○	○	S
Always see Q and A posts mod/forum:viewqandawithoutposting	⊙	○	○	○	
View subscribers mod/forum:viewsubscribers	⊙	○	○	○	
Manage subscriptions mod/forum:managesubscriptions	⊙	○	○	○	
Throttling applies mod/forum:throttlingapplies	⊙	○	○	○	S

[Save changes] [Cancel]

5. For the setting **Start new discussions**, select **Prevent**.
6. Click the **Save changes** button.

In Moodle, permissions at a lower context override permissions at a higher context. For example, by default the role **Student** has the permission for **Start new discussions** set to **Allow**. However, you could set this for **Prevent** for a specific course, and because a course is a lower context than the entire site, for that course the permission **Prevent** will override the site wide setting of **Allow**. A single activity, such as this forum, is the lowest context in Moodle. Overriding permission in a single activity will not affect anything else; it affects only that activity.

Moodle's online help has a good discussion of the differences between **Inherit, Allow, Prevent**, and **Prohibit**. It also describes how conflicts between permissions are solved by the software. If you're going to use **Override roles** elsewhere in Moodle, read this section of the help.

Keeping Discussions on Track

One of the biggest challenges in using forums for an online class is keeping discussions focused on the topic. This becomes even more difficult when you allow students to create new topics in a forum. Moodle offers two tools that you can use to help keep discussions on track: custom scales and splitting discussions.

Use a Custom Scale to Rate Relevance

Moodle enables you to use a scale to rate student work. A scale offers you something other than a grade to give the student as feedback. Scales can be used to rate forum postings, assignment submissions, and glossary entries. The following screenshot shows a feedback on the relevance of a posting, given in a custom scale by a teacher:

To create and apply a custom scale, follow these steps:

Users with the roles Administrator, Course creator, and Teacher can create custom scales.

1. From the **Administration** block, click on **Scales**. This displays the **Scales** page.

2. On the **Scales** page, click on the **Add a new scale** button. This displays the **Editing scale** page.

3. On the **Editing scale** page:

   ° Enter a **Name** for the scale. When you apply the scale to the forum, you will select the scale by this name.

   ° In the **Scale** box, enter the items on your scale. Separate each item with a comma.

   ° Write a **Description** for your scale. Students can see the description, so use this space to explain how they should interpret the scale.

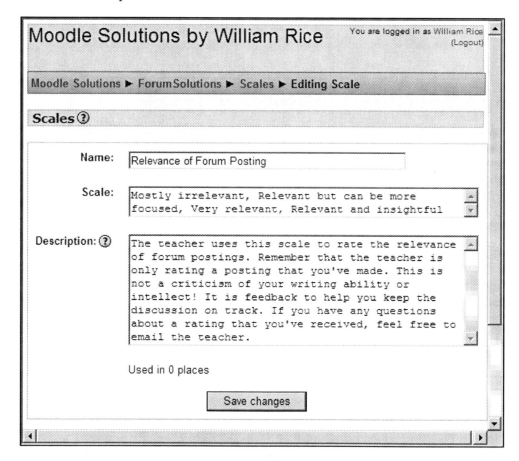

4. Select the **Save changes** button. You are now ready to apply the scale.

5. Create or edit the forum to which you want to apply the scale. The key setting on the **Editing Forum** page is **Allow posts to be rated?**

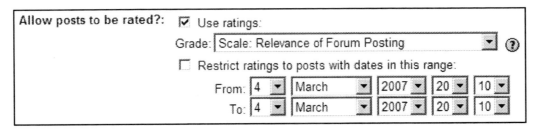

6. When you review the student postings in the forum, you can rate each posting using the scale you created, as shown as follows:

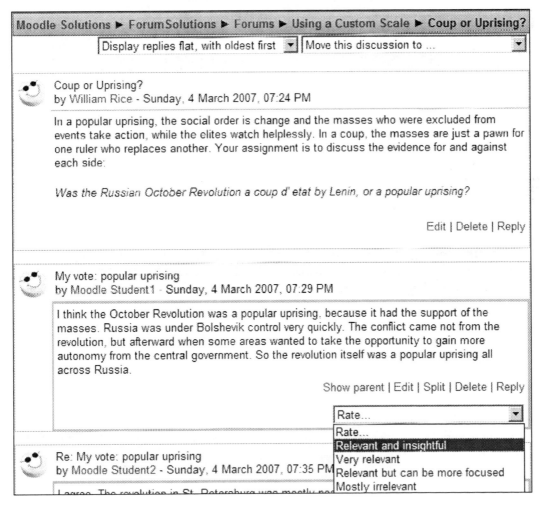

7. When you finish rating the postings, click on the **Send in my ratings** button at the bottom of the page to save your ratings.

Split Discussions

Users with the role Administrator, Course creator, or Teacher can split a discussion. When you split a discussion at a post, the selected post, and the ones below, become a new topic.

Note that you cannot take a few posts from the middle of a topic and split them into a new discussion. Splitting takes every post that is nested below the selected one and puts it into a new topic.

Before the Split	After the Split
Topic 1	New Topic 1-2
Reply 1-1	Reply 1-2-1
Reply 1-2	Reply 1-2-2
Reply 1-2-1	Reply 1-2-3
Reply 1-2-2	Topic 1
Reply 1-2-3	Reply 1-1
Reply 1-3	Reply 1-3
Reply 1-4	Reply 1-4
Reply 1-4-1	Reply 1-4-1
Reply 1-4-2	Reply 1-4-2

Will Splitting Change the Meaning?

Splitting a thread can rescue a conversation that has gotten off topic. However, it can also change the meaning of the conversation in ways that you don't expect or want.

Note that in the example above, after the split, the new topic is moved to the top of the forum. Will that change the meaning of your forum? Let's look at an example. Following is the screenshot showing the first topic in a forum on the October Revolution of Russian history. In this topic, students discuss whether the revolution was a coup or a popular uprising:

	Add a new discussion topic			
Discussion	**Started by**	**Replies**	**Unread ✓**	**Last post**
Coup or Uprising?	William Rice	3	0	Moodle Student3 Sun, 4 Mar 2007, 07:41 PM

The teacher made the first posting, and several students have posted replies. Some of these replies, as shown in the following screenshot, favor the theory that the revolution was a coup, while others that the revolution was a popular uprising:

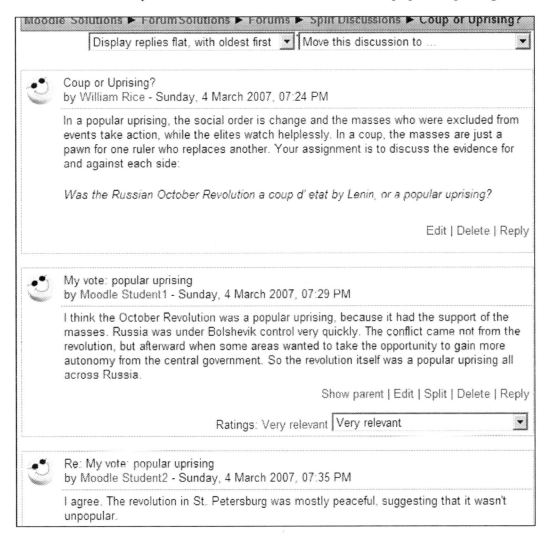

Note that the posting by Student2 is a *reply* to the posting by Student1. You might have missed that because the reply is not indented. That's because the teacher has selected **Display replies flat**. If the teacher had selected **Display replies in nested form**, you would see Student2's reply indented, or nested, under Student1's reply. We can tell that Student2 is replying to Student1 because the subject line indicates it is a reply to Student1 (**Re: My vote: popular uprising**).

The first two postings are pro-uprising. The last posting is pro-coup. It occurs to the teacher that it would facilitate discussion to split the forum into pro-uprising and pro-coup topics.

The teacher scrolls down to the pro-coup posting, which just happens to be the last posting in this forum, and clicks on **Split**, as shown in following screenshot:

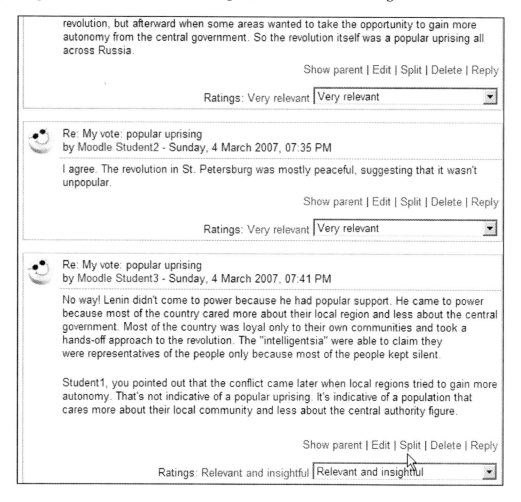

This will make a new topic out of the pro-coup posting:

Discussion		Started by	Replies	Unread ✓	Last post
Coup		Moodle Student3	0	0	Moodle Student3 Sun, 4 Mar 2007, 07:41 PM
Coup or Uprising?		William Rice	2	0	Moodle Student2 Sun, 4 Mar 2007, 07:35 PM

Will Splitting, Move Replies You want to Keep in Place?

In this example, the teacher was lucky. Under the pro-coup posting, there were no pro-uprising replies. If there were, those replies would have come with the pro-coup posting, and the teacher would not have been able to make a topic that was completely pro-coup.

As the split function takes all of the replies nested under the split point, when a discussion has gone off course and come back on course, you should consider whether you really want to split. Consider the example below. In Reply 1-2, the conversation went off topic. For the next two replies, it remained off topic. But then, Reply 1-2-3 brought the conversation back on topic. Should you split the conversation at Reply 1-2? If you do, you'll move Reply 1-2-3, which is on topic, out of Topic 1. When it's taken out of Topic 1, will Reply 1-2-3 still make sense?

Before the Split	After the Split
Topic 1	Reply 1-2 (off topic)
Reply 1-1	Reply 1-2-1 (off topic)
Reply 1-2 (off topic)	Reply 1-2-2 (off topic)
Reply 1-2-1 (off topic)	Reply 1-2-3 (back on topic)
Reply 1-2-2 (off topic)	
Reply 1-2-3 (back on topic)	Topic 1
Reply 1-3	Reply 1-1
Reply 1-4	Reply 1-3
Reply 1-4-1	Reply 1-4
Reply 1-4-2	Reply 1-4-1
	Reply 1-4-2

Before splitting a forum thread, consider these two issues:

- How will rearranging the topics change the meaning of the forum?
- Will splitting move any replies that you want to keep in place?

Monitoring Student Participation in a Forum

One of the most important tasks that you face when managing a forum is determining which students are participating, and which are not. Moodle gives you several ways to get this information.

Who has Posted to a Forum?

Moodle's log files can tell you who has participated in an activity. We will look at how useful log files are in determining which students have posted to a forum.

In order to view the list of students who have posted to a forum, follow these steps:

1. Enter the course for which you want the report.

2. From the **Administration** block, select **Reports**.

3. Under **Choose which logs to see**, select the settings for the:

   Course you want to see. It will be set to the course you are in, but you can choose a different course.

   Participants. Leave this set to **All participants** so that you see the log for all students in the course.

   Dates of the activity. To see who has ever posted to a forum, leave this set to **All days**.

   Activity. In this case, it is the forum named **Using a Custom Scale**.

   Actions. In this case, it is **Add** a posting to the forum.

   Display of the information. In this case, I will display the report on screen. You can also download it as a text or Excel file.

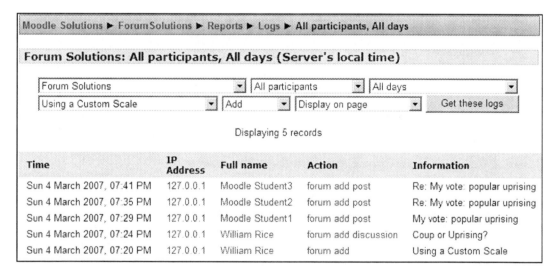

4. Click on the **Get these logs** button. The students that have posted to the forum will be displayed.

What Postings has a Student Made?

In the above method, we started with the forum and displayed which students had contributed to it. You can also start with the student, and see what that student has posted to any forum.

To see the postings that a student has made to all forums in a Moodle site, follow these steps:

1. Enter the course for which you want the report.

2. From the **People** block, select **Participants**. A list of the students, teachers, and course creators for this course is displayed.

3. Select the student whose forum postings you want to see. The student's public profile page is displayed.

4. Select the **Forum posts** tab, as shown in the following screenshot. Under this tab, you will see two sub-tabs: **Posts** and **Discussions**.

5. The **Posts** sub-tab displays all the replies the student has contributed to forums on this site. The **Discussions** sub-tab displays all the new topics (new discussions) the student has contributed.

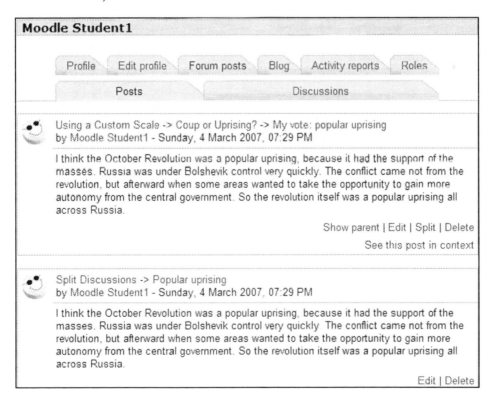

6. The **Activity reports** tab displays all the activities the student has engaged in on the entire site. It has several sub-tabs. The **Outline report** is easier to read, and also shows you all the forums that the student is enrolled in, and has posted to.

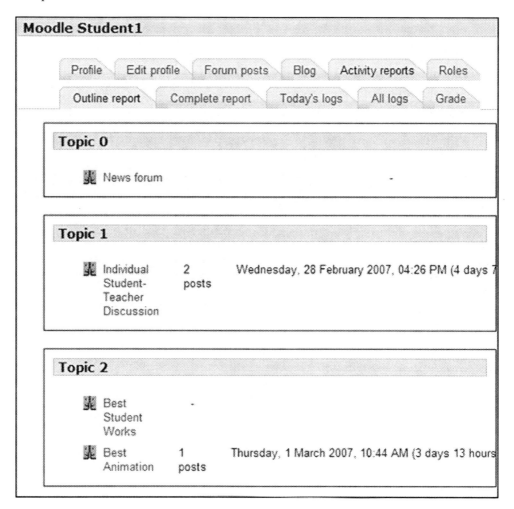

Summary

Forums are one of Moodle's strongest features. Don't be constrained by the traditional view of forums, just as a place for group discussion. You can also use a forum for one-to-one discussion between a student and an instructor.

We saw how a custom scale can be used to rate the relevance of postings; you can also use custom scales to have student rate any otehr aspect of a forum posting. For example, suppose your class were writing a play. You could have students contibute story ideas and character sketches to a forum. Then, the class could use a custom scale to vote on whether to incude them in the play.

In calsses that require student participation, Moodle's log files can quantify a student's participation in class discussion. Splitting a discussion can bring it back on track, when it has been taken over by an unintened subject.

Whenever you need to involve students in a discussion, a Moodle forum offers a place for student and teachers to have a productive discussion.

3
Chat Solutions

Trying to use online chat to compensate for a lack of face-to-face contact in a course is like trying to use soy in a dish that calls for meat: it's a poor substitute. However, chat has some unique advantages that face-to-face contact doesn't have. The key to making the best use of Moodle's, or any LMS's chat function, is to use chat in a way that takes advantage of its unique strengths, instead of trying to make it act like a face-to-face meeting. To continue our metaphor: you can't make soy taste like steak, but you can make some delicious dishes from it.

In this chapter, we explore the questions such as *What is chat good for?*; *How can I achieve success in an online chat?* As Moodle's chat function is similar to most other chat software, the answers to these questions apply to more than just Moodle.

Uses of Chat

What is chat good for? If we want chat to be more than just a substitute for face-to-face meetings, what can we do with it? That is the subject of this section.

Test Preparation and Online Study Groups

For some students, an online class can feel very isolated. This is especially true for those of us who grew up before the age of online bulletin boards, instant messaging, and short text messages. As midterm and final exam time approaches and the student's stress level increases, this feeling of isolation can grow. Using chat sessions for review and test preparation can reduce the feeling of isolation and can be an effective teaching method. Also, the chat logs provide a unique learning tool, that you won't get in a face-to-face review session.

Creating Study Groups

One of the keys to a successful chat session is limiting the number of participants. If you are teaching a large class, consider breaking the class into groups and holding a review session for each group. Moodle enables you to separate any class or specific activity into groups. The members of one group cannot participate in the activities of another group. So, when you separate your class into groups, you've essentially created a separate chat for each group. The groups can be totally separate, so that the members of each group cannot even see each others' work, or, be visible to each other, so that the members of one group can see but not participate in all the other groups' work.

Groups Carried Over to Other Activities

When you create a group in Moodle, it exists at the course level. This means the group can be applied to all activities within the course and not outside.

If you separate the students into groups for a chat, and then use those groups in other activities, the students will have the same group in those other activities. Before separating students into groups for a chat, you should consider the effect the grouping will have on any other activity in the course.

If you want to use different groups for different activities, you will need to either:

- Change the group membership as needed. That is, change the groups as you progress through the course.
- Create a second course, enroll your students in the second course and create alternative groups and activities in that course.

Key Settings for Study Groups in Chat

The key settings in the **Editing Chat** window are:

- **Save past sessions**, which determines how long the chat transcript is saved.
- **Everyone can view past sessions**, which enables the students to view the transcripts.

- **Group mode**, which when set to **Visible groups**, enables different groups to view each others' transcripts.

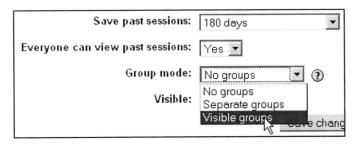

Assigning Review Topics

If the study group has not worked together before, you might want to jump-start their relationship by assigning each student in the group a different review topic to prepare for the chat. You should also prepare review questions to ask each student during the chat. Remember that in an online chat, it's very easy for students to "lurk" and watch without participating. You need to be ready to draw them out with questions about the review material that you've assigned.

What Kind of Questions?

Typing is more difficult than speaking and people naturally take the path of least resistance. Keep your questions open-ended and encourage students to elaborate, so that they do not give one word answers, which is an easy way out.

Reviewing Papers and Other Assignments

Regrettably, the internet has made plagiarism easier than ever. Moodle can't be used to determine if a paper or passage is plagiarized, but a private chat in Moodle can tell you if a student learned anything from the paper of assignment (s)he handed in. The more original a paper, the more the student will remember about it and learn from it. You can schedule a private chat with each student after they've submitted their papers and ask them questions about the subject of their papers.

Making a One-on-One Chat

There are a variety of situations, where you might want to chat one-on-one. Reviewing a student's assignment is one of them. Moodle does not offer an obvious way to limit the participants in a chat to just you and one selected student. Just as we used a workaround in *Chapter 2: Forum Solutions*, to set up a private forum for one student and the teacher, we need to use a workaround here to set up a private chat.

Workaround 1: Using Groups

The workaround for creating a one-on-one forum involved using the Groups feature. Moodle enables you to create a separate chat for each group in a class. We can create a group for every single student in our class and then create a chat with the groups. If we select **Separate groups** for the **Group mode**, we will totally segregate each student into his or her own chat room, where only that student and the teacher can participate and see the transcript. This would be appropriate if the students should not see each others' papers. If we select **Visible groups** for the **Group mode**, we will limit the chat room to just the student and teacher, but, other students will be able to see the transcript. This would be appropriate if the students could see each others' papers.

Workaround 2: Hiding the Chat

Another way to keep a chat room private is to hide the chat after the desired participants are in the chat room. In this case, you would schedule a chat time with the designated student. In the screenshot that's coming up, you can see that **William Rice** and **Moodle Student2** have entered the chat room. At that point, William Rice clicks the **Update this Chat** button to enter the **Editing Chat** page.

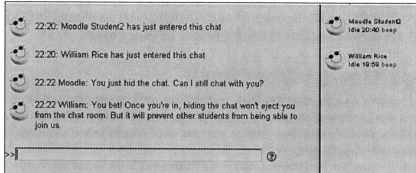

Then, on the **Editing Chat** page, for the **Visible** setting, select **Hide**.

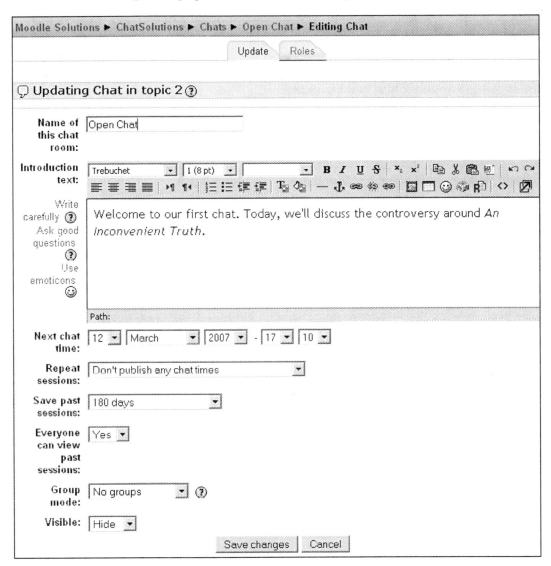

The chat will now be hidden from other students. You and the student who have already entered will remain in the chat.

Guest Speakers

Chat gives you a chance to have a guest speaker in your online course. You'll need to create a student-level account for your guest speaker. When you're creating the speaker's account, as a matter of courtesy, set the **Email display** setting to **Hide my email address from everyone**, unless your guest speaker explicitly gives permission for students to contact him/her via email.

You will also need the speaker's permission to save the chat session for future viewing. This is to avoid copyright issues. Try to get this in writing from the speaker.

For a good example of a chat transcript featuring a guest speaker, see:
`http://www.netsquared.org/2006/conference/remote`.

Including Chats from Previous Classes

The **Save past sessions** setting, saves a transcript of each chat session. You can use these transcripts as reference material in your classes. To get the transcript from a past chat into your class, use the Backup function to export the chat from the previous class, and the Restore function to bring it into your current class.

Copying a Transcript

The procedure for copying a transcript of a chat from a past course into a current course is as follows:

1. Enter the past course as a **Teacher** or **Administrator**.
2. From the **Administration** block, select **Backup**.
3. On the **Course backup** page as shown in the next screen shot, select the chat whose transcript you want to copy. At the bottom of the page, select **Yes** for **Course files**. If the students in your current course are different than those in the past course, do not select **User Data**.

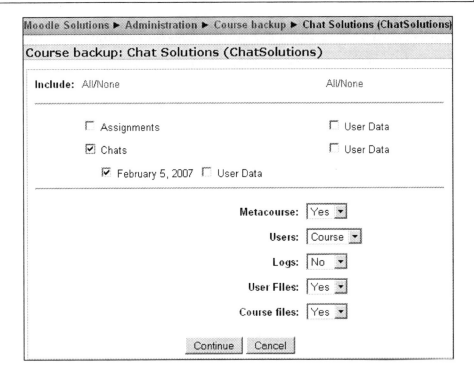

4. Click on the **Continue** button, Moodle will prompt you to confirm your settings, and the name of the backup file. The file will be saved in the Course Files folder.

5. Conveniently, Moodle opens the Course Files folder for you, and you can immediately restore the backup up chat to your current course as shown in the following screenshot:

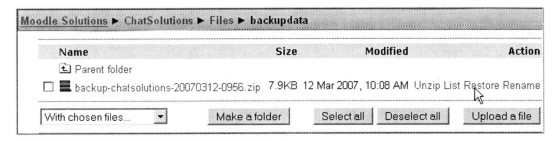

The **Everyone can view past sessions** setting, enables students to view the transcripts of past chats. This means that you can save the chat transcripts from previous classes and use them as reference material in the future. However, the very presence of a chat room in your course means that students can enter the chat room at any time and engage in a chat session. How do you include the transcript of a past chat in your course, without creating an active chat room? The answer is Moodle's **Override Roles** function.

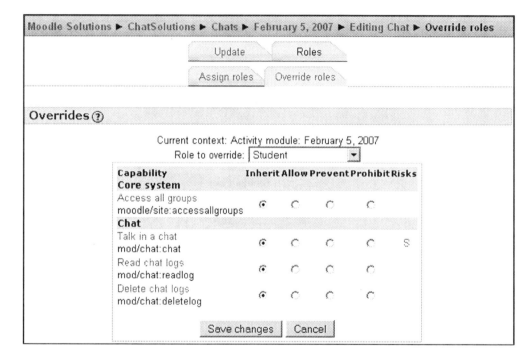

From the **Editing Chat** window, select **Override roles**. By default, the **Student** role is permitted to the **Talk in a chat** option. Selecting **Prevent** for this capability will disable the student's permission to talk in the chat room, while still allowing them to **Read chat logs**.

Foreign Language Practice

You can use chat rooms to pair up students with foreign language speakers, for language practice. A chat room offers several unique advantages for language practice:

- First, a chat enables students to reach out to another country in ways they might not be able to without the chat.

- Second, a chat's pace is usually faster than most written exercises, yet slower than face-to-face conversation. In a chat, the student has extra, but not too much time, to translate what his/her foreign partner said, and to think about what to say next. A chat's pacing makes it a good transition between leisurely-written exercises and fast face-to-face exchanges.

- Third, chat logs provide material for review and remediation. After the chat, each student can review their own or another student's transcript for grammar, spelling, and vocabulary. For instructions on how to accomplish this, see the *Compiling and Reviewing Chat* section later in this chapter:

Preparation for Foreign Language Chat

One of the keys to a successful foreign language chat is preparing the students' vocabulary. Before the chat, agree upon the topic with your foreign counterpart. Prepare your students by building their vocabulary in that topic. Also, give the students a list of keystrokes for foreign language characters. Feel free to copy the following table, for your students.

Typing Foreign Language Characters

Hold down the *Alt* key, and type the four digits on your keyboard, not the numeric keypad. When you release the *Alt* key the foreign language character will appear.

á	Alt+0225	à	Alt+0224	â	Alt+0226	ä	Alt+0228
å	Alt+0229	Á	Alt+0193	Ã	Alt+0195	Ä	Alt+0196
Å	Alt+0197	À	Alt+0192	Â	Alt+0194	æ	Alt+0230
Æ	Alt+0198	ç	Alt+0231	Ç	Alt+0199	ê	Alt+0234
é	Alt+0233	ë	Alt+0235	è	Alt+0232	Ê	Alt+0202
Ë	Alt+0203	É	Alt+0201	È	Alt+0200	ï	Alt+0239
í	Alt+0237	î	Alt+0238	ì	Alt+0236	Í	Alt+0205
Ì	Alt+0204	Î	Alt+0206	Ï	Alt+0207	ñ	Alt+0241
Ñ	Alt+0209	œ	Alt+0156	Œ	Alt+0140	ô	Alt+0244
ö	Alt+0246	ò	Alt+0242	õ	Alt+0245	ó	Alt+0243
ø	Alt+0248	Ó	Alt+0211	Ô	Alt+0212	Õ	Alt+0213
Ø	Alt+0216	Ö	Alt+0214	Ò	Alt+0210	š	Alt+0154
Š	Alt+0138	ú	Alt+0250	ü	Alt+0252	û	Alt+0251
ù	Alt+0249	Ù	Alt+0217	Ú	Alt+0218	Ü	Alt+0220
Û	Alt+0219	ÿ	Alt+0255	Ÿ	Alt+0159	ý	Alt+0253
Ý	Alt+0221	ª	Alt+0170	Þ	Alt+0222	þ	Alt+0254
ƒ	Alt+0131	ß	Alt+0223	µ	Alt+0181	Ð	Alt+0208

Compiling and Reviewing Chat Transcripts

You can take several approaches for reviewing chat logs. One of the easiest approaches is to have students copy a minimum number of lines from their chat logs into an online assignment and edit these in the assignment window. Or, you can copy lines from the various chats yourself and compile them into a document that you ask the students to edit online. This enables you to choose the chat portions that offer the greatest opportunity for learning.

Moodle's `Assignment` module gives you an easy place to present the transcript and instruct the student to edit it.

Copying Chat Transcripts

In order to copy a chat transcript in Moodle, as you select the text you will also select the avatars (pictures) of the participants and the time of each posting. Refer to the screenshot displaying chat transcripts:

You might not want to include the avatars and times in the transcript. To create a copy of the transcript without these, do the following:

Select the part of the chat transcript that you want to copy, as shown in the previous screenshot and follow the procedure:

1. Press *Ctrl-C* or *Apple-C* to copy.

2. Open a new word-processing document. For example, open a new Microsoft Word document.

3. From the **View** menu, select **Normal** (for Word) or **Draft** (for WordPerfect) or **Web Layout** (for OpenOffice). The key is to view the document so that it wraps as few lines as possible. In many word processors, viewing the document in draft mode minimizes the number of lines that are wrapped.

4. From the **Edit** menu, select **Paste special.** At this point, most word processors will give you a dialog box with several choices. Select **Unformatted text**.

5. The chat transcript will be pasted into the word processing document, without the avatars; just the text is pasted.

6. At this point, if you are in Word, you can use a trick to easily select the times at the beginning of each line. With the *Alt* key held down, draw a rectangle around the characters that you want to select. Your selection can include just the first few words of each line, shown as follows:

```
→   22:43 Student1··Well,·let's·see,·we·have·on·the·bags,·Who's·on·first,·What's·on·second,·I·Don't·Know·is·on·third...¶
→   22:43 Student2··That's·what·I·want·to·find·out.¶
→   22:43 Student1··I·say·Who's·on·first,·What's·on·second,·I·Don't·Know's·on·third.¶
→   22:43 Student2··Are·you·the·manager?¶
→   22:44 Student1··Yes.¶
→   22:44 Student2··You·gonna·be·the·coach·too?¶
→   22:44 Student1··Yes.¶
ı   22:44 Student2··And·you·don't·know·the·fellows'·names?¶
→   22:44 Student1··Well·I·should.¶
ı   22:44 Student2··Well·then·who's·on·first?¶
→   22:45·Student1··Yes.¶
```

7. Delete the selected text. Now you will be left with just the chat participant's names and their dialog.

8. Copy the chat and paste it into the Moodle assignment.

Assigning a Chat Transcript as an Editing Exercise

After you have compiled chat transcripts, you can assign students the task of editing them for spelling, grammar, vocabulary, and logic. This is especially useful in a language course, after your students have participated in a foreign language chat. You can then compile parts of the chat transcripts into an assignment, and have the students find and correct any mistakes that they or their foreign partners made.

Tips for a Successful Chat

Preparation is the key to a successful chat session. Here are some things that you and your students can do to help make your chats easier and more productive.

Basic Chat Etiquette

Before the first chat, consider giving your students a short handout with some basic etiquette instructions. You can even include these in the chat announcement. For example:

1. If you can, wait for the moderator or speaker to ask for your questions.

2. If you want to ask a question and it cannot wait, send a "?" and wait for the moderator or speaker to acknowledge you. This is the online equivalent of raising your hand.

3. If you have a comment or observation, send a "!" and wait for the moderator or speaker to acknowledge you. When the speaker reaches a good place to pause, (s)he will invite you to comment.

4. If you need multiple lines, use "..." at the end of a line to indicate there's more coming. Without the "..." at the end of a line, other participants assume that you have finished what you have to say.

5. Just as in email, uppercase is considered "shouting.", and, it's more difficult to read than normal mixed case. So, avoid it.

6. Give others time to respond to your last message. Sending messages in a rapid sequence, without giving others a chance to respond, can make the chat feel more like an interrogation than a conversation. Also, when you do get a response to one of your rapid-fire questions, you might not be able to tell which question the person is responding to.

7. Don't judge the other person on their typing skills. Lots of smart people can't type well. Especially those of us who grew up writing our term papers by hand.

8. Think before hitting *Enter*. The class which you are attending might save the chat transcript for a long time. The person whom you just offended might copy the chat and save it for even longer.

9. Use humor carefully. Without facial expression and tone of voice, humor—especially sarcasm—often translates poorly online. For example, you can say "You gotta be kidding!" in person and make it clear by your tone and expression that you're teasing the other person. Online, it can just as easily be translated as "You're stupid!".

10. If you want to convey an emotion online, and you're not confident that your text alone will accurately communicate the mood, consider using *smileys*. These are graphics that you can insert into your text to show the mood of a statement.

11. The table that follows shows you how to type smileys. Note that you type the characters without spaces between them.

Smiley	Mood	Type this	Smiley	Mood	Type this
☺	smile	:-)	☹	sad	:-(
☺	big grin	:-D	☻	shy	8-.
☺	wink	;-)	☺	blush	:-I
☺	mixed	:-/	☺	kiss	:-X
☺	thoughtful	V-.	☺	clown	:o)
☺	tongueout	:-P	☺	black eye	P-|
☺	cool	B-)	☺	angry	8-[
☺	approve	^-)	☺	dead	xx-P
☺	wide eyes	8-)	☺	sleepy	|-.
☺	surprise	8-o	■	evil	}-]

12. If you're stepping away from the chat, please send a message to indicate so. Moodle doesn't enable you to set your "status" like many instant message programs do. So, you need to inform your fellow chatters when you step away and come back to the chat.

Prepare for a Definite Starting and Ending Time

"Start and end on time" is good advice for any class. For an online chat, it is especially important. If a face-to-face class starts late, you can keep the students engaged with conversation until the class starts. Most students will not walk out of the room, and when class does start, they will be there ready to participate. If an online chat starts late, you will have no idea if a participant has walked away from his/her computer while waiting for the chat to start and if/when (s)he will return. In an online chat, a late starting time can make your students lose intrest more easily, than in a face-to-face classroom.

You can help prevent this by coming to the chat prepared with some pre-chat material. This is material which you can use for discussion before the chat begins, but that is not essential for the chat. For example, you might spend a few minutes asking the students about their experience level with online chats, or whether their navigation through the course is clear. Or, find some interesting or outrageous trivia about the chat subject, and quiz the students about it, until all the participants have arrived.

Limit the Number of Participants

Moodle's default Chat module lacks some advanced features that you would use to help manage a large chat. For example, some chat applications enable you to "whisper" to another user, that is, to send them a private message. If a student wants to ask the teacher a question, without interrupting the chat, (s)he can whisper that question to the teacher. Some chat applications also have a "raise your hand" function, that enables a student to let the moderator know that (s)he wants to speak. And for very large chats, the ability to enable only one person at a time to speak is also very useful. As Moodle's chat module is being developed, these capabilities might be added. But for now, the best way to keep a chat under control is to limit the number of participants.

If you must conduct a chat with a large number of participants, here are a few tips for managing the chat:

- Make the chat window as large as possible, so that you can see as much of the chat history and participants as possible.
- The chat should be actively managed by the moderator. The moderator should:
    - Restate the topic at the beginning of the chat.
    - Bring off-topic posts back on topic.

    °   Issue a number to each participant, and require participants to answer in order. Participant number 2 doesn't click the **Send** button until participant number 1 has posted a comment, and so on.

Prepare a Greeting for Latecomers

Students might enter the chat at different times. When a student enters a Moodle chat, that person sees only the transcript going forward; the student doesn't see what has already been said in the chat room. If you have a welcome message for students as they enter the chat, you'll need to repeat it each time a student enters the chat. Keep this message in a text file where you can quickly copy and paste it into your chat window.

If your greeting is several paragraphs long, you should be aware that Moodle's chat window does not recognize the *Enter* character. So if you paste two or more paragraphs into the chat window, they will be recognized as one long paragraph. Instead, use *Shift-Enter* to create hard-line breaks between the paragraphs.

Focus

Chatting online requires more effort than talking. Limit the chat session to one specific topic or activity, and stick to it. Students should come prepared to discuss one topic or complete one task only. As the moderator, you should be prepared to keep the chat on-topic. Unless brainstorming and expanding, the topic is part of the chat's goals, you should respond to off-topic postings by bringing them back on-topic. This lends structure to the chat session and helps students stay focused.

Insert HTML

You can insert HTML code into your chat. This is useful for sharing links, embedding graphics, and formatting text in your chat. To insert a link, just type the web address. In a chat, links that you type, become automatically clickable. This is shown in the following screenshot:

You can insert images by placing them into the standard HTML image tag. If the image is on the Web, include the full link to the image. For example, typing `http://farm1.static.flickr.com/172/427149859_037a0a9202.jpg` into a chat line, produces the following:

Summary

In this chapter, we learned that, online chat has some unique advantages over an in-person classroom discussion. Students do not need to deal with the fear of public speaking. Transcripts can be edited and used as course material, and conversation can proceed at a leisurely pace. This gives participants time to think.

The key to using these advantages is preparation. Prepare your students by ensuring that they know chat room etiquettes and how to use the software. Prepare yourself by having material ready to copy and paste into the chat. Also, everyone should be prepared to focus on the goals and subject of the chat. More than any other online activity, chat requires that the teacher takes on a leader's role and guides the students to a successful learning experience.

4
Quiz Solutions

A quiz can be more than just a test. At its best, a quiz can also become a learning experience. Moodle offers features that help you to accomplish that. This chapter gives you different ways of using Moodle quizzes for more than just testing.

Distribute Quizzes Over Time

Distributed practice is when a student practices a skill or knowledge during many sessions that are short in length and distributed over time. For example, if you're teaching a language course, you might practice every day for one week on a list of vocabulary words. That would be distributed practice. But even more effective would be repeating that practice once a week for the next few weeks.

Advantages and Limitations of Distributed Practice

Students who use distributed practice learn more material, and remember the material longer, than students who cram because:

- It's easier for students to maintain motivation and focus for short spans of time rather than for an all-night study session.
- Short practice sessions prevent mental and physical tiredness. Fatigue interferes with memory and reasoning, and reduces the ability to focus.

Research indicates that we continue to learn and process information that we study, after the study period has ended. If our brains were ovens, you could say we continue to "bake" the knowledge for a while even after the heat has been shut off. The more practice sessions we engage in, the more times we experience this effect.

Several factors affect how well, distributed practice works:

Factor	Effect on Distributed Practice
Length of the practice session.	The shorter the better. It should be just long enough to cover the material, but not long enough to fatigue the student.
Time between practice sessions.	Research shows that at first, the time between sessions should be short enough so that students don't forget the material between practice sessions. As the students gain proficiency and confidence with the material, the time between sessions can be increased. There are no hard-and-fast rules. As a teacher, you must use your judgment and monitor the students' performance, adjusting the time between sessions as needed.
Time period over which practice sessions are distributed.	The longer the better. Keep returning to the material until the students master it. Students might demonstrate mastery by performing well on the quizzes you give them, or by using the material in an activity like writing a paper or participating in a forum.

With all this talk of the advantages of distributed practice, there are some situations where massed practice (a long study or work session) is better. For example, when you're writing a paper you often reach a point where you are accomplishing several things at once. You are writing a section now, you have your next few points in mind, you have recalled the next few pieces of information that you need to use, and you know where the piece that you working on fits into the overall organization of the paper. At that point, you do not want to be interrupted. Writers, programmers, artists, and people who do creative work know that sometimes the best way to be productive is to exert a sustained and uninterrupted effort. For each learning situation, you must consider, which would give better results; distributed practice or sustained effort.

Opening and Closing Quizzes at Predetermined Times

The **Editing Quiz** window contains settings that enable you to determine when a quiz becomes available and unavailable to students:

Remember that the show/hide setting determines if a student can see an item in the course or not. So, even when a quiz is closed, students could see it listed in the course. The following table examines how the setting can be used.

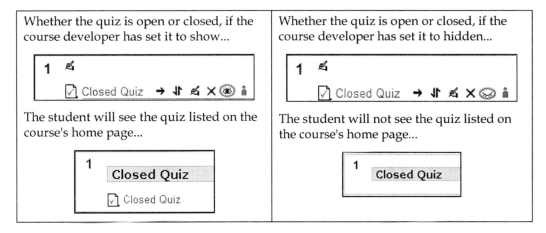

If a student selects a closed quiz, (s)he sees the quiz's description and a message stating when the quiz will open (or when it closed):

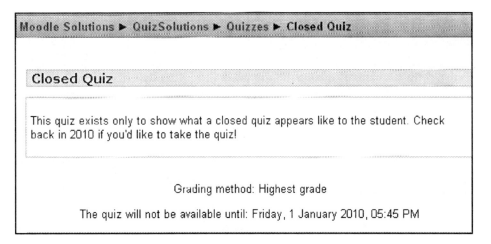

Indicating that a Quiz is Closed

If you're going to close a quiz until a given date, will you allow the student to stumble into the quiz and discover that it is closed until a given date? Or will you indicate to the student that the quiz is closed? You have several options.

In the previous figure, you can see that Moodle tells the student, **The quiz will not be available until: Friday, 1 January 2010, 05:45 PM**. However, that information is not very prominent. Consider using the first line of the quiz's description to explain that the quiz is closed until the open date, so it's the first thing the student reads after selecting the quiz:

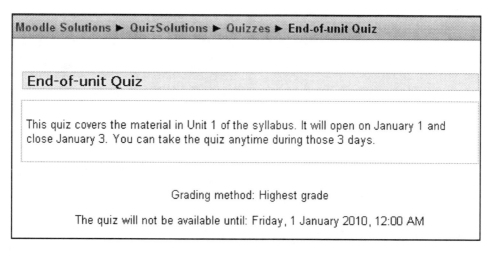

You can use a label on the course's home page to indicate that the quiz is closed, like this:

> The quiz below will open when we finish this topic, on January 1, 2010.
> ☑ End-of-unit Quiz

You can also hide the quiz until it's time for the student to take it.

Use Quizzes for Frequent Self Assessment

Self assessment is the ability of a student to observe, analyze, and judge his or her performance based on criteria that you supply. At its best, self assessment also means that the student can determine how to improve his or her performance. Supplying the students with quizzes that they can take at their own, fulfills the first part of that goal. Using feedback during the quizzes helps fulfill the second. Self assessments are typically not graded. The goal of a self assessment is usually not to achieve a grade, but to practice for a graded activity.

Adding self assessment to your course has several advantages for you and the students. First, self assessments are a chance for students to become more actively involved in their learning. Second, students learn to identify their errors as they make the errors, assuming the self assessment quiz provides immediate feedback. For more about using immediate feedback in a quiz, see *Immediate Feedback Makes a Quiz a Learning Tool*, later in this chapter. This feedback during self assessment reduces the errors students make "when it counts", that is, when they are being graded. Third, self assessments build the students' confidence, and makes them more independent learners, and as a teacher, your workload is reduced by self assessment quizzes that provide feedback, because they reduce the need for you to provide feedback yourself. You can also improve your relationship with your students by showing confidence in their ability to work independently.

Exclude Self Assessment Quizzes from the Gradebook

Moodle gives you a Gradebook for each course. The scores for graded activities, such as quizzes and workshops, automatically appear in the Gradebook. You want a self assessment quiz to display a grade to the student so that (s)he knows how well (s)he did, but, you don't want that quiz grade to be included in the calculation for the student's course grade. Moodle enables you to exclude selected activities from a course's Gradebook.

To exclude the grade for a self assessment quiz from the Gradebook, do the following:

1. From the **Administration** block, select **Grades** (▓ Grades). The first time that a teacher, administrator, or course creator visits a course's Gradebook, the Gradebook displays in its simplest mode:

	View Grades	Set Preferences	
Download in Excel format		Download in text format	

All grades by category ⑦

Student Sort by Lastname Sort by Firstname	Uncategorised Stats		Total Stats		Student Sort by Lastname Sort by Firstname
	points(11)	Percent	points(11) ↓↑	% ↓↑	
Moodle, Student1	-	0%	-	0%	Moodle, Student1
Moodle, Student2	-	0%	-	0%	Moodle, Student2
Moodle, Student3	-	0%	-	0%	Moodle, Student3

2. To exclude a quiz from the grade calculations, you need to view the Gradebook in advanced mode. Select the **Set Preferences** tab. Under this tab, select **Use Advanced Features**, as shown in the following screenshot:

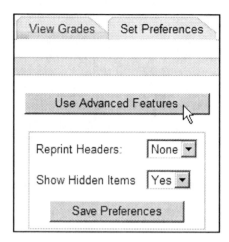

3. Several new tabs appear. Select **Grade Exceptions**, shown in the following screenshot:

4. This page can be tricky. It looks like you should select the activity from the middle column, and then select either **Exclude from Grading** or **Include in Grading** for that item. However, that isn't how this page works. Instead, select the activity from the middle column and then select all of the students whose grade for this activity you want to exclude from the Gradebook. Refer to the following screenshot:

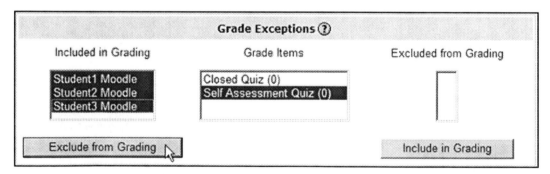

5. And then, select **Exclude from Grading**. This excludes that activity from the selected students' overall grade:

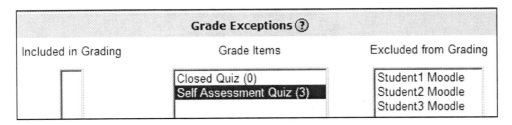

However, note that for the other activity in this course, the Closed Quiz, all of the students' grades will still be included in the Gradebook:

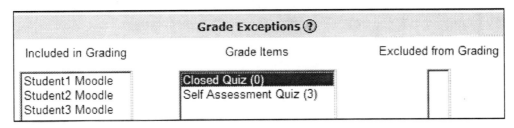

When using this method to exclude self assessment quizzes from the Gradebook, remember that if a student joins your course late, you'll need to return to the **Grade Exceptions** page and exclude that student's self assessment quiz grades from the Gradebook.

Making Quiz—A Learning Tool

In an online environment, immediate error correction almost always takes the form of feedback provided by the learning system. The feedback is a response to a student's answer to a quiz question.

Questions Must be Specific

Immediate feedback is one of the strengths of an e-learning system. One of the weaknesses of an online environment is that the teacher can't ask why the student picked an incorrect answer. The teacher cannot immediately ask the student to discover exactly what information (s)he is missing. For example, this quiz question asks about two items:

In what order should you add the chemicals, and when should they be heated?

If a student gets this question wrong in an online quiz, should the feedback correct the student's knowledge of:

The order in which, chemicals are to be added? or, When to heat them?

There's no way you could know. Break this question into two more specific questions, and then you can design appropriate error correction for each question:

1. In what order should you add the chemicals?
2. The mixture should be heated after which chemical is added?

Online quiz questions must be very specific for immediate error correction to work online. There must be no doubt what item of knowledge is being measured. As feedback is a response to a quiz question, the questions and remedial information must be carefully matched. The quiz question must be specific enough to measure with certainty, what piece of information the student is missing.

Adding Feedback to Quiz Questions

Moodle enables you to create several different kinds of feedback for a quiz. You can create feedback for:

- The entire quiz, which changes with the student's score. This is called **Overall Feedback**, and uses a feature called **Grade Boundary**.
- A **question**, no matter what the student's score on that question. All students receive the same feedback. This is called **General Feedback**, which every question can have.

The type of feedback that you can create for a question, varies with the type of question.

Feedback for a Multiple Choice Question

In a multiple choice question, you can create feedback for correct, partially correct, or incorrect response. If a response has a value of 100%, it is considered completely correct and the student receives all of the points for that question. However, a response can have a value of less than 100%. For example, if a question has two correct responses, you could give each response a value of 50%. In this case, each response is partially correct. The student needs to choose both responses to receive the full point value for the question. Any question with a percentage value between 0 and 100 is considered partially correct.

A response can also have a negative percentage value. Any response with a percentage value of less than zero is considered an incorrect response.

Choosing a response with a value of 100% will display the feedback under **Feedback for any correct answer**. Choosing any response with a point value between 0 and 100% displays the feedback under **Feedback for any partially correct answer**. Choosing any response with a zero or negative percentage displays the feedback under **Feedback for any incorrect answer**. Each response can display its own feedback. This type of feedback is called **Response Feedback**, or just **Feedback**.

The screenshot below shows **Overall Feedback** with **Grade Boundaries**. Students who score 90−100% on the quiz receive the first feedback, **You're a geography wizard...** Students who score 80−89.99% receive the second feedback, **Very good!...**

The screenshot below shows a multiple-choice question that uses several kinds of feedback. You're seeing this question from the course creator's point of view, not the student's. First, you can see **General Feedback: The truth is, most New Yorkers have never even thought about the "missing Fourth Avenue" issue**. After the question is scored, every student sees this feedback, no matter what the student's score.

Below that, you can see that **Choice 1** through **Choice 4** contain feedback for each response. This feedback is customized to the response. For example, if a student selects **Sixth Avenue** the feedback is **Nope, that name is taken. Sixth is also known as the "Avenue of the Americas"**.

Near the bottom of the page, under **Feedback for any incorrect answer**, you can see the feedback the system gives if the student selects one of the incorrect responses. In this case, we use the feedback to tell the student what the correct response is.

There is no feedback under **any correct answer** or **partially correct answer**. Those options are useful when you have multiple responses that are correct, or responses that are partially correct. In this case, only one response is correct and all other responses are incorrect.

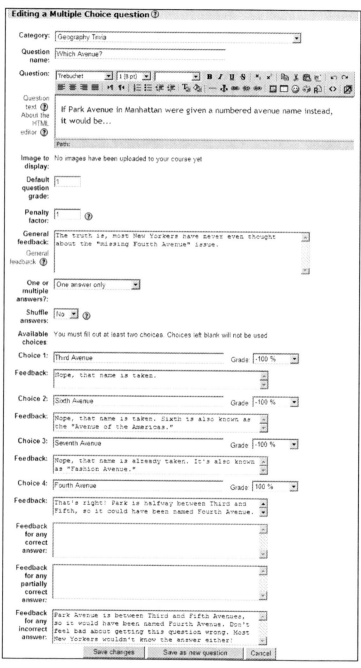

Feedback for a Numeric Question

The next screenshot shows feedback for a question with a numeric answer. Note that the **General Feedback** explains how the question is solved. This feedback is displayed to everyone after answering the question, even those who answered correctly. You might think that if the student answered correctly, (s)he doesn't need this explanation. However, if the student guessed or used a different method than that given in the **General Feedback**, explaining the solution can help the student to learn from the question.

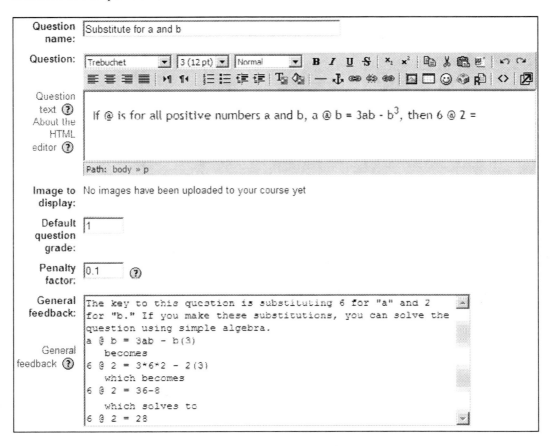

In a numeric answer question, the student types in a number for the answer. This means the student could enter, literally any number. It would be impossible to create customized feedback for every possible answer, because the possibilities are infinite. However, you can create customized feedback for a reasonable number of answers. In this question, I've created responses for the most likely incorrect answers. After I've given this test to the first group of students, I'll need to review their responses for the most frequent incorrect answers. If there are any that I haven't covered, I'll need to add them to the feedback for this question.

| Answer 1: | 28 | Accepted error | | ± Grade: | 100 % |
| Feedback: | Correct. | | | | |

| Answer 2: | -180 | Accepted error | | ± Grade: | None |
| Feedback: | It looks like you transposed the two numbers. In the equation, you substituted 2 for "a" and 6 | | | | |

| Answer 3: | 30 | Accepted error | | ± Grade: | None |
| Feedback: | It appears that instead of calculating b cubed, you calculated b times 3. | | | | |

| Answer 4: | * | Accepted error | | ± Grade: | None |
| Feedback: | No, that answer is incorrect. | | | | |

In the previous screenshot, note that each response has customized feedback. **Answer 1** is correct. **Answer 2** would be the result of switching the two numbers while trying to solve the problem. As this is a likely error, I've included feedback just for that answer, explaining the error the student made. **Answer 3** is the result of interpreting b^3 as "b times 3" instead of "b cubed." This is also a likely error, so I've included feedback for that answer. **Answer 4** is a wildcard, and applies if the student submitted any answer other than the three above.

Reinforce Expertise with Timed Quizzes

Timed quizzes are an example of teaching, using a strategy called **time trials**. Time trials can be used to:

- **Measure** a student's competence at the beginning of a learning unit.
- **Build** a student's confidence with the knowledge or skill.
- **Test** a student's mastery at the end of a learning unit.

Chapter 1 has a section that explains the theory behind time trials in more detail. In general, you should use time trials to build mastery of existing skills and knowledge, and not to build new knowledge. Time trials are a confidence-building technique.

When a student selects a timed quiz, the system displays the time limit for the quiz. You might also want to state the time limit in the quiz's description, as shown in the following screen shot:

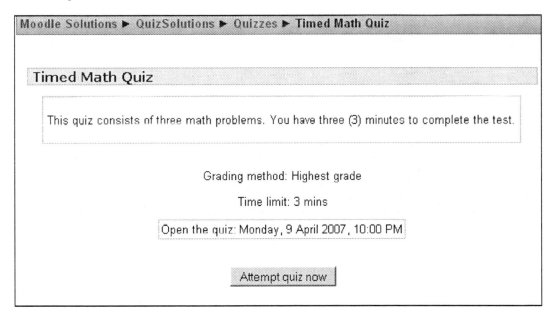

When the student selects **Attempt quiz now**, the student is reminded that the quiz has a time limit:

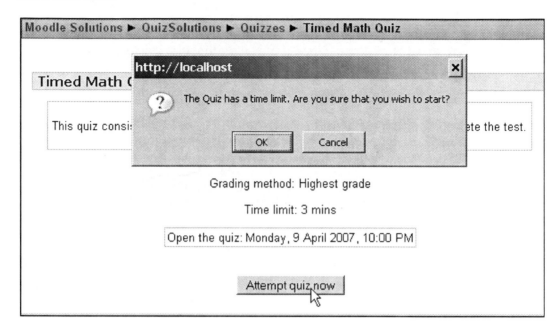

After the student selects **OK**, the quiz displays a timer that appears in a separate floating window, as shown in the following screenshot:

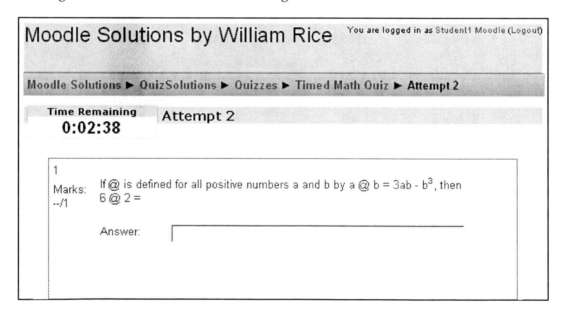

Adding a time limit to a quiz is a matter of changing one setting on the **Editing Quiz** page, as highlighted in the following screenshot:

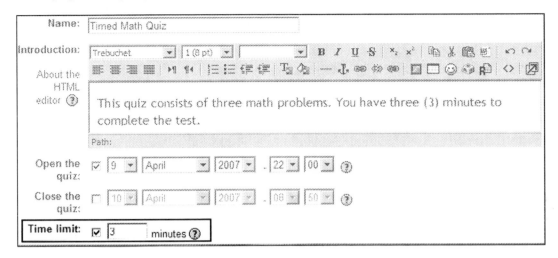

Host a Proctored, Timed Test from a Secure Location

Moodle enables you to restrict the location from which a quiz can be accessed. This is especially useful for a proctored quiz, where you want to be sure that only people in a certain room are able to access the quiz.

This is done with the **Require network address** setting as shown:

Require network address:	64.14.68.15

Only computers that are located at this specified network address can access the quiz.

Different Kinds of Network Addresses

You can specify different kinds of network addresses. Each is explained as follows:

Full IP Addresses

This is the simplest option. Every computer connected directly to the Internet has a unique identifier, called its IP address. Please note the use of the phrase "directly connected", is deliberate and I'll explain it further. A full IP address specifies a single computer, router, printer, or other device on the Internet.

An IP address is specified by writing four numbers, separated by decimal points, like this: 255.255.255.255. Each number can be from 0 to 255. There are a limited number of IP addresses for the Internet. Don't worry, we haven't run out of them yet, and there is a plan for adding more IP addresses.

When you log on to your internet service provider (ISP) from home, your ISP usually gives you an IP address for the time that you are logged on. When you log off, your ISP "takes back" the IP address so someone else can use it. When you log on again, you're given a new one. So, when one of your students accesses the Internet from their homes, (s)he will probably have a different IP address every time. This is important, if you want to restrict a quiz to specific IP addresses. Your students won't be able to access that quiz from their homes. They will need to be physically present at the computers that have the IP addresses you specify.

Often, one IP address serves many computers. Again, think of your home computer. If you have DSL or a cable modem, you probably have a router that enables you to connect several computers to that one modem. In this case, your modem has an IP address. The router enables all of your devices — the computer in your home office, the laptop your kids are using in the living room, the printer you've connected to your router — to share that one IP address. In a similar way, your school or company may have only one IP address that gets shared among many computers. In some modern lecture halls, you will find several wireless access points that students can connect to with their laptops. Usually, each access point will have a unique IP address. In that case, all of the laptops using the access point will share the access point's IP address. The next time you're in a lecture hall, look up at the ceiling; if you see several antennas, each with an IP address written on it, those are the wireless routers.

If you want to use the **Require network address** setting to limit access to a certain room, ask your network administrator if every computer in that room has a unique IP address, or if they share an IP address. If each computer in a room has a unique IP address, you will need to enter the range of IP addresses into this field.

To restrict access to a quiz to one IP address, enter it into the **Require network address** field, like this:

Require network address: 64.14.68.15

To restrict access to a range of IP addresses, enter them like this:

Require network address: 64.14.68.15-20

In this example, the range covers all the IP addresses from 64.14.68.15 through 64.14.68.20.

Partial IP Addresses and Private Networks

In the previous section, I explained that a single router will have a unique IP address, and that the router will share its Internet connection with the computers connected to it. So the router will have a public IP address, like 64.14.68.15. But what about the computers "behind" that router? What IP address will the computers that share the router's Internet connection have?

The area behind a router is considered a **private network**, or **subnet**. The computers on the private network are not connected directly to the Internet; they go through the router. As they're not connected directly to the Internet, they don't need an IP address that is unique to the Internet. Each computer on a private network needs an IP address that is unique within its network, but not unique to the external network. The computers behind a router — the computers on a private network — use the following ranges of IP addresses:

> 10.0.0.0 through 10.255.255.255
>
> 169.254.0.0 through 169.254.255.255
>
> 172.16.0.0 through 172.31.255.255
>
> 192.168.0.0 through 192.168.255.255

If the computers at your school or company have IP addresses that fall within one of these ranges, then your institution is using a private network. For example, if the computers in the room where you want to administer a test have IP addresses from 198.168.0.143 through 198.168.0.162, then those 20 computers are on a private network, and they access the Internet through a router. You can restrict access to just those computers by entering **198.168.0.143-162** into the **Require network address** field.

The diagram on the next page shows two private networks connected to the Internet. Each network sits behind one router, and uses the same range of private IP addresses. The routers have unique IP addresses, but the subnets use the same range of IP addresses.

If the computers in your institution are on a private network, or subnet, entering something like **192.168** or **172.16** into the **Require network address** field will grant access only to those computers on your subnet. If you want to grant access only to computers in a certain room, so that you can proctor the quiz, then find out the IP addresses of the computers in that room and enter the IP address range into the field.

How to Determine a Computer's IP Address

The easiest way to determine a computer's IP address is to ask your network administrator. But if you must do it yourself, here are basic instructions.

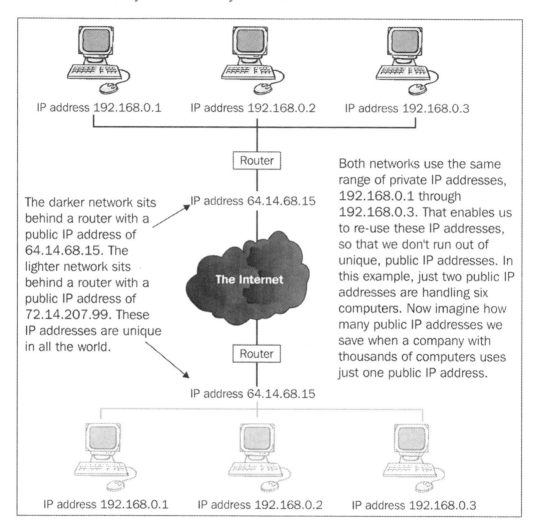

The darker network sits behind a router with a public IP address of 64.14.68.15. The lighter network sits behind a router with a public IP address of 72.14.207.99. These IP addresses are unique in all the world.

Both networks use the same range of private IP addresses, 192.168.0.1 through 192.168.0.3. That enables us to re-use these IP addresses, so that we don't run out of unique, public IP addresses. In this example, just two public IP addresses are handling six computers. Now imagine how many public IP addresses we save when a company with thousands of computers uses just one public IP address.

On Microsoft Windows

From the **Start** menu, select **Run...**

1. In the resulting dialog box, enter **cmd** and then click the **OK** button. A DOS window will appear, like this:

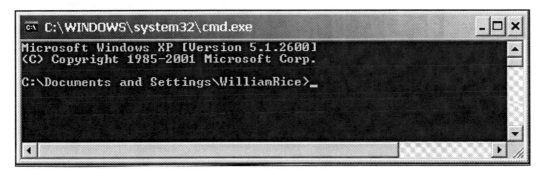

2. If the computer uses Windows 95, 98, or ME, type **winipcfg** and press *Enter*. If the computer uses Windows NT, 2000, or XP, type **ipconfig** and press *Enter*.

3. The IP Address is one of the first pieces of information displayed:

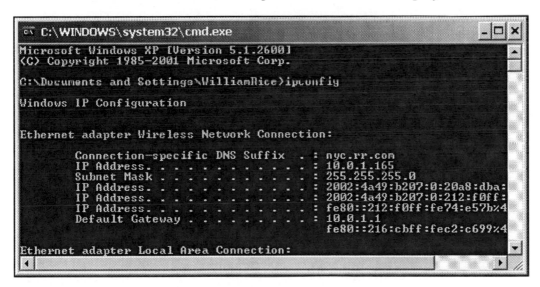

4. To close the window, type **exit** and press *Enter*.

On a Macintosh

- OS X 10.3 or 10.4

    1. From the **Apple** menu, select **Location** and then **Network Preferences...** .

    2. In the Network Preference window, next to **Show:**, select **Network Status**. Your IP address will be listed.

- OS X 10.2

    1. From the **Apple** menu, select **Location** and then **Network Preferences...** .

    2. In the Network Preference window, next to **Show:**, select the method that you use to connect to the Internet. For example, you might be connected via **Built-in Ethernet**, **Internal Modem**, or **Airport**.

    3. After selecting your connection method, click the **TCP/IP** tab. Your IP address will be listed.

- **OS X 10.1 and earlier**

    1. From the **Apple** menu, select System Preferences... .

    2. In the System Preferences window, click the **Sharing** icon. If you don't see this icon, click **Show All** to make it display, and then click **Sharing**. Your computer's IP address will display at the bottom of the window.

- **Mac OS 9**

    1. From the **Apple** menu, select **Control Panels**. A submenu displays.

    2. Select **TCP/IP**. In the TCP/IP window, your IP address is listed.

On a Linux Computer

1. Open a command shell. You might need to refer to your Linux help files or manual to learn how to do this. On most Linux PCs, you can open a command shell with one or two clicks.

2. At the command prompt, type **ifconfig eth0** and press *Enter*. That's a zero, not the letter O, in **eth0**.

3. The system will display the settings for all of the network hardware in your computer. Look for the line that begins with **inet addr:**. Your IP address will be listed immediately after that.

Summary

In this chapter, you saw how to use Moodle's `Quiz` module to create self-assessment and learning experiences. Some of the features we explored are:

- Opening and closing quizzes at predetermined times.
- Scoring quizzes without including them in the students' final grade.
- Feedback for quizzes, questions, and individual responses to questions.
- Timed quizzes.
- Restricting access to a quiz, based on the student's location.

There are other features that you can use to make a quiz a good learning experience. For example, you can use the settings for **Attempts allowed** and **Each attempt builds on the last** to enable students to try a quiz several times. After each attempt, the student can retain the correct answers and work at the wrong answers. You can use **Adaptive mode** to create questions that allow multiple attempts immediately after the student has entered an answer, and that change their feedback according to the student's answer. I encourage you to explore these and other features. With the right approach, perhaps we can change things enough so the words test and quiz no longer scare so many students, but are something that they look forward to.

5

Lesson Solutions

A Moodle lesson can be a powerful combination of instruction and assessment. Lessons offer the flexibility of a web page, the interactivity of a quiz, and branching capabilities. A lesson consists of a series of web pages. Usually, a lesson page contains some instructional material, or a question about some material the student just viewed.

Coming up is a screenshot of an instructional lesson, and appears like any normal web page:

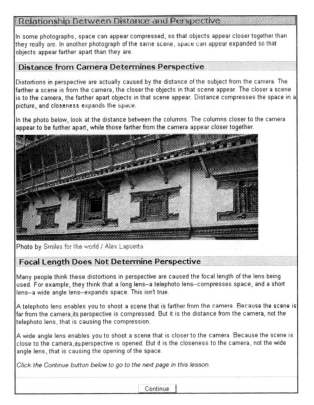

Relationship Between Distance and Perspective

In some photographs, space can appear compressed, so that objects appear closer together than they really are. In another photograph of the same scene, space can appear expanded so that objects appear farther apart than they are.

Distance from Camera Determines Perspective

Distortions in perspective are actually caused by the distance of the subject from the camera. The farther a scene is from the camera, the closer the objects in that scene appear. The closer a scene is to the camera, the farther apart objects in that scene appear. Distance compresses the space in a picture, and closeness expands the space.

In the photo below, look at the distance between the columns. The columns closer to the camera appear to be further apart, while those farther from the camera appear closer together.

Photo by Smiles for the world / Alex Lapuerta

Focal Length Does Not Determine Perspective

Many people think these distortions in perspective are caused the focal length of the lens being used. For example, they think that a long lens--a telephoto lens--compresses space, and a short lens--a wide angle lens--expands space. This isn't true.

A telephoto lens enables you to shoot a scene that is farther from the camera. Because the scene is far from the camera, its perspective is compressed. But it is the distance from the camera, not the telephoto lens, that is causing the compression.

A wide angle lens enables you to shoot a scene that is closer to the camera. Because the scene is close to the camera, its perspective is opened. But it is the closeness to the camera, not the wide angle lens, that is causing the opening of the space.

Click the Continue button below to go to the next page in this lesson.

Continue

The "jump question" is used to test a student's understanding of the material. If you get it right, you proceed to the next item, and if you get it wrong, you're either taken back to the instructional page or jump to a remedial page. However, the jump question could just as easily ask a student what (s)he is interested in learning next, or some other exploratory question.

When the student clicks on the **Continue** button, at the bottom of the lesson page, (s)he is taken to a question page, shown next:

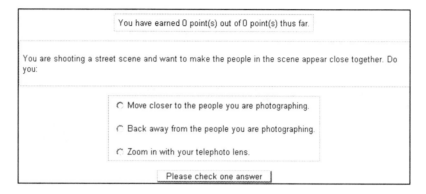

Each answer displays a different feedback:

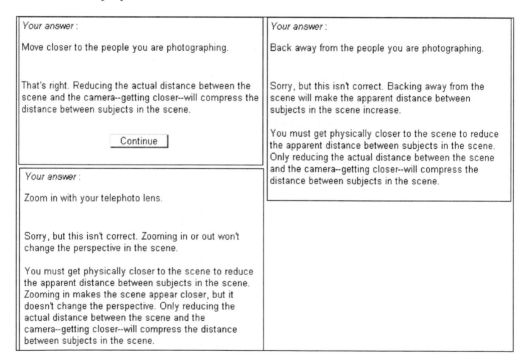

If the student answers correctly, (s)he is taken to the next instructional page. An incorrect answer takes the student to a remedial page.

Remedial: Compressing Perspective

In the photo below, the space between each of the marchers in the front row is the same:

Photo by Celeste Hutchins.

Look at the two men closest to you. You can see that the space between them is over four feet. If one of them reached out his arm, he could not touch the other:

This is the normal sequence for a lesson in Moodle. Later, we'll discuss how we can make the best use of the Lesson module.

Moodling Through a Course

Moodle enables students to view resources and complete the activities in any order. As long as the resources and activities are available to the student, the student can access them at any time, and in any order. A paragraph from www.moodle.com, explains its approach to e-learning:

The word Moodle was originally an acronym for **Modular Object-Oriented Dynamic Learning Environment***, which is mostly useful to programmers and education theorists. It's also a verb that describes the process of lazily meandering through something, doing things as it occurs, an enjoyable tinkering that often leads to insight and creativity. As such it applies both to the way Moodle was developed, and to the way a student or teacher might approach studying or teaching an online course.*

Need for Sequential Activities

We don't want our students to "meander" or wander through course items. We want to enforce a specific order of resources and activities. One of the most-requested features in Moodle is the ability to require students to complete their activities in a given sequence. This ability is often called **activity locking**, which the official Moodle documentation wiki defines as:

 A conditional activity is a dependency filter that prevents a student from entering and/or seeing an activity, resource, section, or some other Moodle course feature. Typical conditions are based on an overall score, on a specific activity and time spent on it.

For example, a student will not see the second topic until they have scored 80% or higher on the first topic's quiz.

As of this writing, Moodle's latest version (1.9) does not have activity locking as part of its core. Version 2.0, due in late 2007, is scheduled to support activity locking as part of its core. Until then, you can obtain a variety of add-on modules that enable you to use activity locking (see http://docs.moodle.org/en/Activity_Locking). On a smaller scale, you can use the Lesson module to create learning experiences that students must complete in a given order.

Activity Locking versus Sequential Lessons

Activity locking can be used to lock the student out of any kind of resource or activity. It affects an entire course. It can be used to restrict and guide a student's progress from one resource or activity to another, based upon the student's score and/or time spent on viewing something.

Within a lesson, you can restrict and guide a student's progress through a series of web pages. The path through the lesson pages is based upon the student's answer to a question at the end of each page, but outside the lesson, the student is free to go anywhere in the course.

For the purpose of enforcing a sequence of activities, a lesson is much more limited than activity locking. However, the Lesson module comes with Moodle's core distribution. If a lesson can accomplish the kind of sequential learning that you need to create, you will find it much easier than adding and using one of the activity locking modules.

The Lesson module offers a kind of activity locking, which could enable/disable access to a lesson, dependent on a student's performance in another lesson. For example, you can lock the student out of Lesson 2, until (s)he has completed Lesson 1. Imagine a course consisting of mostly lessons. You could use the "dependent on" feature to enforce a given order to the lessons. You could also add web pages, forums, links, and other items to the course that the student can access at will. By mixing dependent lessons and regular Moodle items, you can have the best of both worlds: Lessons and lesson pages that must be completed in order, and other course resources that can be accessed at any time. With these tools at your disposal, you might not need to use an add-on module for activity locking, or to wait for Moodle's core distribution to support activity locking.

Lesson Settings

In this section, I'll go through the **Editing Lesson** page from top to bottom. I'll discuss most of the settings, and focus on the ones that are most useful for creating the effect of a deck of flash cards. So, by the end of this section, you will understand how, most of the settings on the **Editing Lesson** page affect the student's experience. In later sections, I'll discuss how to use these settings to create specific kind of experiences. For example, in the section, *Use a Lesson to Create a Deck of Flash Cards*, I'll discuss the settings that are especially useful for making a lesson behave like an online deck of flash-cards.

General Settings

At the bottom of each question page in a lesson, you can place a quiz question. **Maximum number of answers/branches** determines the maximum number of answers that each question can have. If each answer sends the student to a different page, then the number of answers is also the number of branches possible. For a flash card experience, you will probably use True/False questions, and set this to **2**. After creating question pages, you can increase or decrease this setting without affecting the questions that you have already created.

This is shown in the following Screenshot:

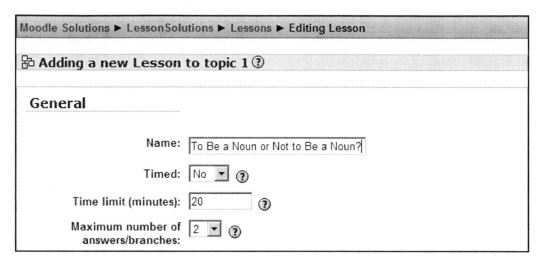

Grade Options

If a lesson is being used only for practice, most of the grade options are irrelevant.

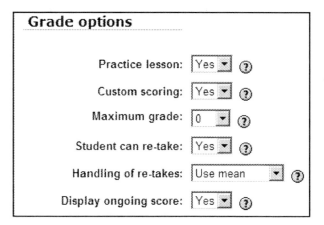

In the screenshot above, if you set **Practice lesson** to **Yes**, this lesson will not show up in the Gradebook. And, if you set **Maximum grade** to **0**, the lesson does not appear in any of the Grades pages. Either way, the student's score in this lesson will not affect the student's final grade in the course.

Flow Control

Some of the options under **Flow control** makes the lesson behave more like a flash card deck. The other options become irrelevant when a lesson is used for flash cards.

Allow student review, enables a student to go backwards in a lesson, and retry questions that (s)he got wrong.

Look at the setting for **Action after correct answer**. Note, that in this case it is set to **Show an unanswered Page**. That means that after a student answers a question correctly, Moodle will display a page that the student either hasn't seen or that (s)he answered incorrectly. The **Show an unanswered Page** setting is usually used during a flash card lesson, to give the student a second chance at answering questions correctly. During a normal lesson, you will usually use, **Allow student review** to enable students to go back to the questions they got wrong.

Display review button, displays a button after the student incorrectly answers a question. The button allows the student to re-attempt the question. If your questions have only two answers (true/false, yes/no), then allowing the student to retry a question immediately after getting it wrong doesn't make much sense. It would be more productive to jump to a page, explaining why the answer is wrong, and use the **Show an unanswered Page** setting to give the student another chance at the question, at a later time.

Maximum number of attempts, determines how many times a student can attempt any question. It applies to all questions in the lesson.

Minimum number of questions, sets the lower limit for the number of questions used to calculate a student's grade on the lesson. It is relevant, only when the lesson is going to be graded.

Number of pages (cards) to show determines, how many pages are shown. If the lesson contains more than this number, the lesson ends after reaching the number set here. If the lesson contains fewer pages than this number, the lesson ends after every card has been shown. If you set this to zero, the lesson ends when all cards have been shown.

Lesson Formatting

The settings under **Lesson formatting** are used to turn the lesson into a slide show, which appears in a pop-up window. The **Slide Show** setting creates the slide show window. **Slide show width, Slide show height,** and **Slide show background color,** set the format of the slide show.

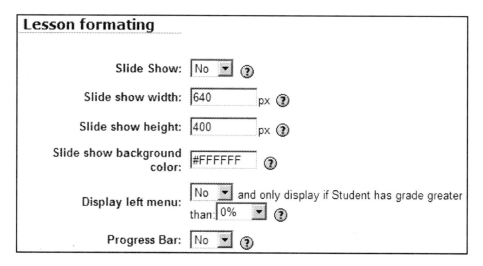

Display left menu, displays a navigation bar on the left side of the slide show window. The navigation bar enables the student to navigate to any slide. Without that navigation bar, the student must proceed through the slide show in the order that Moodle displays the lesson pages, and must complete the lesson to exit (or the student can force the window to close). Sometimes, you want a student to complete the entire lesson in order, before allowing him or her to move freely around the lesson. The setting for **and only display if Student has grade greater than** accomplishes this. Only if the student achieved the specified grade, will (s)he see the navigation menu. You can use this setting to ensure that the student goes completely through the lesson the first time, before allowing the student to freely move around the lesson. The **Progress Bar** setting displays a progress bar at the bottom of the lesson.

Access Control

Recall that, at the beginning of the chapter we learned that lessons are the only activity that can be made dependent on completing another activity. That is, you can require that the student completes a specific lesson in your course before allowing the student to access the current lesson. Now, look at the **Dependent on** setting in the screenshot:

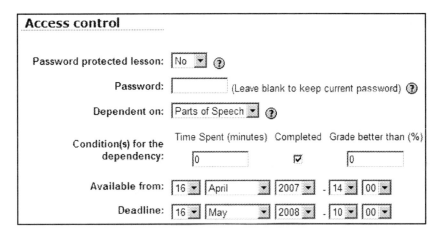

Before the student can access this lesson, (s)he will need to complete the lesson **Parts of Speech**. As of now, in Moodle's standard distribution, this is the only kind of activity that supports this type of activity locking.

Other Lesson Settings

The **Other** settings area, has some settings that can make the lesson more interesting for the student.

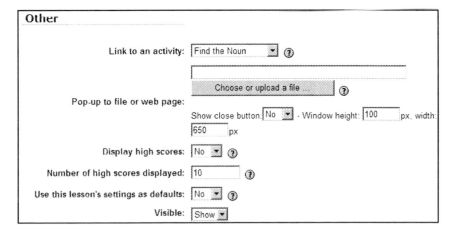

Notice in the screenshot, **Link to an activity** is set to **Find the Noun**. This setting places a link on the last page of the lesson to the activity or resource specified. The drop-down list contains all of the resources and activities in the current course. The user must click the link to be taken to the location. So, this setting doesn't force the user to proceed to a specific place after the lesson.

The **Choose or upload a file...** setting enables you to specify a file that is displayed in a separate window, at the beginning of the lesson. This can be useful if you want the student to refer to something during the lesson. For example, you could display a diagram and present a series of lesson pages that refer to that diagram. Be careful about combining this with the **Slide show** setting from the previous screenshot. If you use them both, you'll have Moodle displayed in one window, the file displayed in another, and the slide show lesson displayed in a third window.

Display high scores lets the high scoring students choose a name to post their scores under. This setting doesn't do anything, if you make the lesson a **Practice lesson**.

Controlling the Flow through a Lesson: Instructional Pages, Questions, and Remedial Pages

If your lesson questions have all true/false or yes/no answers, you will probably set **Maximum number of answers/branches** to **2**. If you use more than two answers per question, consider whether you want to create a jump page for each answer. If you do create a unique jump page for every answer on the question pages, and you use three answers per question, how many cards will there be in your flash card deck? The answer: your lesson will have three pages for each flash card, the card itself, plus two jump pages for remedial information.

The illustration shows this kind of lesson flow.

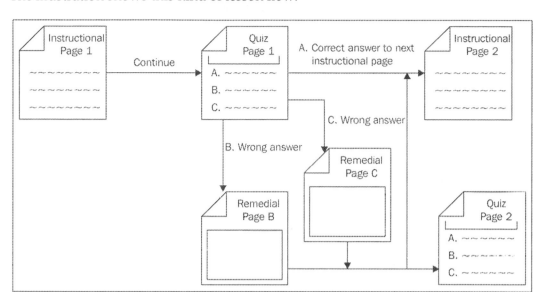

We don't want to spend all day creating a short lesson. But, we still want to show remedial information when a student selects the wrong answer. Consider phrasing your questions, answers, and remedial pages so that one remedial page can cover all of the incorrect responses. The illustration shows this kind of flow. Note that we've reduced the number of remedial pages that have to be created.

If you must give a different feedback for each answer to a question, consider using a quiz instead of a lesson. In Chapter 4, the section *Adding Feedback to Quiz Questions* shows you how to create a feedback for each individual answer in a quiz question. While a remedial page in a lesson can consist of anything that you can put on a web page, a feedback can only consist of text. However, quizzes are usually easier to create than lessons. If a quiz with feedback will suffice, you can probably create it faster than the kind of branching lesson shown in the figure. But if your feedback must be feature-rich, there's nothing better than Moodle's Lesson module.

Use a Lesson to Create a Deck of Flash Cards

Flash cards are a classic teaching strategy. In addition to a learning experience, flash cards also make a good self-assessment tool for students. You can use a lesson, as if it's an online deck of flash cards. One advantage of using an online system is that, log files tell you if a student completed the flash card activity, and how well the student did.

Keep it Moving

Students are accustomed to a flash card activity moving quickly. Showing a remedial page after each incorrect response will slow down the activity. Consider using only question feedback, without remedial pages in between cards.

In a flash card lesson, every page will be a question page. In a lesson, a question page can have any content that you can put on a normal web page. So each page in your flash card lesson can consist of a fully-featured web page, with a question at the bottom, and some text-only feedback for each answer.

When setting the jumps for each answer on the question page (on the card), make sure that a correct answer takes the student to the next page and an incorrect answer stays on the same page. Again, this duplicates our physical experience with flash cards. When we get the answer right, we move on to the next card. When we get the answer wrong, we try again until we've got it right.

Lesson Settings that Help Create a Flash Card Experience

For a flash card lesson, you will probably set **Practice lesson** to **Yes**, so that the grade for this lesson will not show up in the Gradebook. As stated above, setting **Maximum grade** to **0** will also prevent this activity from showing up in the Gradebook. However, it will also prevent the student from seeing his or her score on the activity. If you want the student to see how well (s)he did on the lesson, set **Practice lesson** to **Yes** and use a maximum grade that makes sense, such as one point per correct answer.

Allow student review enables a student to go backwards in a lesson, and retry questions that (s)he got wrong. In a flash card activity, this is usually set to **No**. Instead, we usually set **Action after correct answer** to **Show an unanswered Page**. That means that after a student answers a flash card question incorrectly, Moodle might display that card again during the same session. If the student answers the question correctly, that card is not shown again during the same session. This is how most of us are accustomed to using physical flash cards.

Number of pages (cards) to show determines how many pages are shown. You usually want a flash card session to be short. If the lesson contains more than this number, the lesson ends, after reaching the number set here. If the lesson contains fewer than this number, the lesson ends, after every card has been shown. For a flash card lesson, set this to less than the total number of cards.

You can use the **Slide Show** setting to display the lesson in a separate window, and make that window the size of a flash card. This can help to create the effect of a deck of cards.

When the student uses a physical deck of flash cards, (s)he can see approximately how far into the deck (s)he is. The **Progress bar** setting can help to create this effect with your online deck of flash cards.

Use an Ungraded Lesson to Step through Instructions

In Chapter 1, I introduced an instructional strategy called pre-correction. Briefly, pre-correction is anticipating mistakes that students might make, and providing instruction to help the student avoid those mistakes. For example, you give the students a complex assignment. You know that even if you supply them with written instructions, they are likely to make mistakes, even when following the instructions. You might also give the students a video demo, and a **Frequently Made Mistakes** document (FMM). You could even host a chat before the assignment, to answer any questions they have about how to complete it. If you focus these items on the parts of the assignment that are most likely to cause trouble, they become examples of pre-correction.

You can use a lesson to give students pre-correction for difficult instructions. Place directions that should be read in a specific order on a series of lesson pages. See to it that the students step through those pages. This has several advantages over placing all of the instructions on one page. They are as follows:

- Moodle will log the students' view of the lesson pages, so that you can confirm, they read the instructions.

- While the length of a lesson page is unlimited, the tendency when creating them is to keep them short. This encourages you to break up the directions into smaller chunks, which are easier for students to understand.

- You can insert a question page after each step, to confirm the user's understanding of the step. Question feedback and remedial pages can correct the student's understanding, before they move to the next step.

If you use this technique, the lesson should probably be a **Practice lesson**, so that the students' grade doesn't affect their final grade for the course.

Spot Students who are having Trouble

One of the challenges of online teaching, is spotting a student who is having trouble with the material. In a classroom, the student's expression, body language, and tone enable an observant teacher to identify when the student is having trouble. Online, we don't have these indicators. So, we must use lessons, quizzes, chats, and other activities to constantly monitor the student's progress.

You cannot drill down into the lesson and see which questions an individual student got wrong. You can do this for a quiz, but not a lesson. Therefore, if you want to use a lesson to check a student's understanding of a topic, you must make that topic very specific. For example, suppose a lesson covers three topics: The Writing of the United States Constitution, The Virginia Constitution, and The Beliefs of George Mason. If you see that a student scored low on the lesson, you would be unable to see which topic(s) gave the student trouble because you can't see the scores obtained for individual questions. For assessment purposes, it would be better to break that lesson into three very specific lessons, and link them using the **Link to an activity** setting.

A Workaround

Lessons are designed to primarily be a teaching tool, and only secondarily an assessment tool. However, if you decide that you prefer to use a lesson for assessment, you can work around this limitation. This workaround enables you to determine if a student answered incorrectly on an initial question, or on a remedial question. A low score on remedial questions should prompt action on the teacher's part, such as contacting the student and offering additional help.

You have seen how a lesson usually consists of an instructional page followed by a question page, and that when a student answers a question incorrectly the lesson can display a remedial page. After the remedial page, you can present another question on the same topic. Now, imagine a lesson that covers three items. Each item has its own instructional page followed by a question page, and a remedial page followed by another question page. So not counting the entry and exit pages, there would be:

- Three topic pages
- Three question pages
- Three remedial topic pages
- Three remedial question pages

If you were looking at the Gradebook for this lesson, and a student's grade, indicated that (s)he got two questions wrong, could you determine whether it was because (s)he gave:

- One incorrect response on two of the items.
- Two incorrect responses for the same item.

If the student answered incorrectly on both the first and the remedial questions for the same item, it could indicate, the student is having trouble with that item. But the Gradebook won't tell you that. You will need to drill down from the Gradebook into the lesson to see that student's score for each question. From the Gradebook, you would select the category in which the lesson is placed.

In this example, I have not categorized my activities:

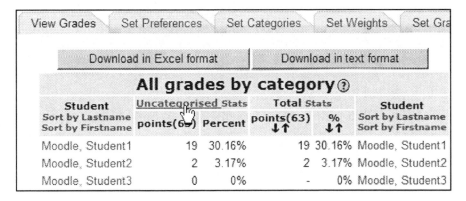

After selecting the category (or just **Uncategorised**), a table of grades for each student/activity displays this:

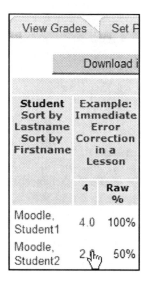

I see that Student2 did not score well on the lesson. So I select the student's score to drill down into the lesson. I select the **Reports** tab, then the **Overview** sub-tab, and then the grade that I want to investigate:

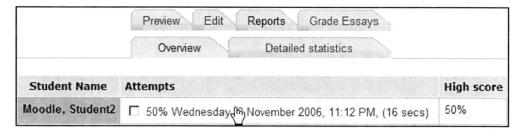

Finally, I think that I'm going to see a detailed report telling me which questions this student got right or wrong. Then, I'll be able to determine which concepts or facts (s)he had trouble with, and help the student with those items. But instead, I see this:

Attempt: 1		
Student:	Student2 Moodle	
Time taken:	16 secs	
Completed:	Wednesday, 8 November 2006, 11:16 PM	
Raw grade:	2/2	
Grade:	50%	

Multiple Choice: Question: Compressing Distance	Class statistics
Question: You are shooting a street scene and want to make the people in the scene appear close together. Do you:	
Answer:	
☑ Zoom in with your telephoto lens.	42.86% checked this one.
☐ Move closer to the people you are photographing.	42.86% checked this one.
☐ Back away from the people you are	14.29%

Notice that the top part of the page tells me the same thing as the previous page. This student scored 50% on the lesson. The bottom part of the page doesn't tell me which questions this student missed. Instead, it gives me statistics for how the class answered each question. That would help me determine, how many students had trouble with a certain question. But it doesn't help me determine which questions this student had trouble with. Unfortunately, there is no way for me to find out how the student answered each lesson question. *Moodle records the final grade, but not each answer.* Even if I go into Moodle's database, and look at the table **mdl_lesson_grades**, I see only final scores and not individual question scores. This student's attempt is recorded in the second row of the table shown in the screenshot:

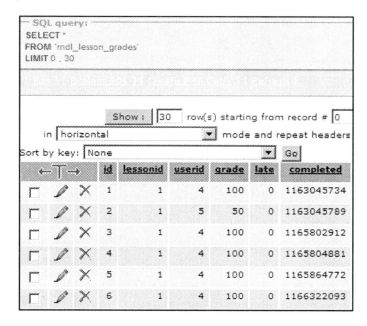

I seem to have arrived at an impasse. I want to know whether Student2 had trouble with some initial questions and then got them correct after remediation, or if Student2 had trouble with both the initial and remediation questions for a single item. However, Moodle doesn't store Student 2's responses to individual questions, only the student's final score. So I will improvise.

The screenshot below shows a remedial question from the lesson. Recall that in the lesson I created, a remedial question only displays when the student has answered a question incorrectly. Please note that on this remedial question, the correct answer is worth '1' point, and each incorrect answer is worth '0' points, as shown in the following screenshot:

Question: Expanding Space ⇕ ✑ 🔍 ✕

You are shooting the interior of an apartment, and want to make the living room appear more spacious. You have a normal and a wide-angle lens. Do you:

Multiple Choice

Answer 1: Stand outside the room, and shoot through the doorway with a normal lens.

Response 1: Sorry, this is incorrect. Remember, compressing and expanding the apparent space in a photo is all about the distance between the scene and the camera. So if you want to expand the space in this photo, choose the option that gets you closest to the subject: stand inside the room, and shoot it with the wide angle lens.

Score 1: 0

Jump 1: End of lesson

Answer 2: Stand outside the room, and shoot through the doorway with the wide angle lens.

Response 2: Sorry, this is incorrect. Remember, compressing and expanding the apparent space in a photo is all about the distance between the scene and the camera. So if you want to expand the space in this photo, choose the option that gets you closest to the subject: stand inside the room, and shoot it with the wide angle lens.

Score 2: 0

Jump 2: End of lesson

Answer 3: Stand just inside the room, and shoot it with the wide angle lens.

Response 3: That's right. Compressing and expanding the apparent space in a photo is all about the distance between the scene and the camera. So if you want to expand the space in this photo, choose the option that gets you closest to the subject: stand inside the room, and shoot it with the wide angle lens.

Score 3: 1

Jump 3: End of lesson

Now suppose, my lesson has five instructional pages, each followed by a question page and possibly a remedial instructional page and then a remedial question. If the scores for correct answers are all set to 1 and for incorrect answers are all set to 0, the maximum score is 5 and minimum is 0. However, for a less-than-perfect score, I can't tell if the student answered incorrectly on the remedial questions.

Now, suppose I give a score of '-10' for getting a remedial question wrong. What would happen to the student's overall score for the lesson if (s)he missed a remedial question? It would be negative, and I would be able to spot the students having real trouble with the concept being taught. If I make the score for each incorrect answer on the remedial questions a large negative number, I can easily spot the students who are not being helped by the remedial instructional pages.

There is a disadvantage to this method: the last page of the lesson will display the student's grade. What effect would it have on a student's morale to see that his or her score on the lesson is '-20'?

Once again, we need to improvise. Specifically, we need to ensure the student never sees the last page of the lesson. We can do this by creating our own end-of-lesson page.

Create a page that informs the student that (s)he has reached the end of the lesson. On this page, place a link to the course's home page, or wherever you want the student to go after the lesson. Instruct the student to click this link to exit the lesson. Moodle will still display a Continue button at the bottom of the page, which takes the student to the last page. Therefore, your instructions should emphasize that the student should click the link and not the Continue button, and that the Continue button will display an "invalid grade."

Summary

Lessons are a flexible tool for creating both instructional and assessment experiences. The key to making best use of them is planning. When creating a lesson, plan the flow within the lesson. Know which jumps you want to make before you start creating the lesson, and plan how you want to combine the lesson with other activities into a larger flow. For example, many users favor a flow that puts a non-interactive, reading or viewing activity first, then an interactive lesson, followed by a quiz, and finally a chat or forum for review.

Since a lesson offers both presentation and question capabilities, it is tempting to try to make it do the work of both a web page and a quiz. However, a lesson functions best when used as a bridge between those two resources. Don't be afraid to experiment with using lessons in new ways. Let us know about your experiences on the official www.moodle.org user forums.

6
Wiki Solutions

We usually think of a wiki as a group activity that students engage in, on their own schedule. A wiki is a powerful tool for collaboration, and it does enable students to participate in a group activity from anywhere, and at any time. However, a wiki can also be a powerful tool for individualized learning, called **differential learning**. It means that the learning experience should be customized for each student. With individual wikis, you can differentiate the learning experience for your students.

Use a Wiki to Relate Material to Big Ideas

In Chapter 1, I introduced the concept of using Big Ideas as a teaching strategy. Briefly, big ideas are the organizing principles and core concepts of a discipline. Big ideas bring order to a course by giving the course a theme for organizing it. As a useful organizing tool, a big idea must be more specific than a one-word concept, such as *Democracy*. However, it must also be broad enough to apply to a variety of topics. The continuous struggle of various groups to gain human and civil rights would be specific enough for a big idea, while still being applicable to a variety of topics. You will probably need a few big ideas to adequately organize a year's worth of instruction.

A big idea must enable the student to organize information, and to find relationships among the information learned during a course. At its best, a big idea also helps the student to relate what is learned in the course to his or her own life. This process of organizing information around a big idea, and relating it to other information and one's life, requires thought and effort from the student. A class wiki can be a good tool for recording these thoughts.

During the course, students can use a wiki to relate new knowledge back to the big ideas. So, set aside a wiki for the big ideas and pre-populate it with them. If there are several big ideas, consider creating an initial page for each big idea. Then, as each topic is covered, require the students to add to the wiki beneath the appropriate big idea(s). The additions should relate the acquired knowledge back to the big idea.

I'm assuming that the *Big Idea Wiki* will be open to the entire class. That will make it a collaborative project. If you prefer, you can keep this activity private between the individual and the teacher.

Why a Wiki?

Moodle offers several tools that students can use for a repeated writing assignment, with instructor feedback. Forums, journals, and blogs are also good options. So why use a wiki? In this section, I'll explore the reasons to use a wiki for relating course material back to the big ideas. My primary goal isn't to convince you that I'm right, but to present you with all the factors you need to make a good decision for your course and your students. If we arrive at different conclusions, that's fine.

Why not a Forum Instead?

For integrating knowledge into a big idea, wikis have several advantages over forums as explained below:

- The first advantage applies only if you want the big idea wiki to be an individual activity. In the current version of Moodle, there is no way to create a private forum for just one student. Everyone who uses the forum can see all the postings, even if they can't edit them. There is a workaround for this, but it is labor-intensive. That is, you will have to create a separate group for each student in your course. The next step would be to create a forum with the **Group mode** set to **Separate groups**. This will limit the use of the forum to just the individual student, and the teacher. However, forums are not meant to be a place where just one individual records his/her thoughts, and just one individual responds (you, the teacher). If you want each student to think and record his/her thoughts independently, a forum might not be the best choice.

- Second, remember that one of the purposes of using a big idea is to provide a unifying theme for course material. If you devote a forum topic to one big idea, then at the end of the course, you will have a collection of forum postings about that big idea. But, if you create a wiki page for a big idea, then at the end of the course you have a single document devoted to that big idea. I feel that a wiki's structure does more to encourage the production of unified knowledge than a forum does. For example, one of your students' most popular online resources will be www.wikipedia.org, and not forumpedia.org.

- Third, your students' understanding of how new knowledge relates to the big idea can change drastically during a course. A wiki enables, and encourages, repeated editing of an entry. The entry grows and changes as the student's understanding changes. In a forum, the student would need to create a new reply each time his/her understanding changes. A forum offers a good history of the student's changing understanding. However, the wiki's format does a better job in presenting the current state of your students' understanding.

Would a Journal do it?

What we've described in the previous topic is focused journal writing. That is, writing periodically about your changing understanding of a topic. Moodle's Journal module would seem to be the right choice. However, it has three disadvantages.

- First and most importantly, when a student updates a journal, the new entry replaces the old entry. To put it another way, a journal activity has only one entry, which is updated each time the student edits it. Unlike a paper journal, in a Moodle journal, the student cannot look back at previous entries to review his/her changing understanding of the topic. A wiki's **History** tab enables you to see the student's previous writing.

- Secondly, the Journal module is being deprecated in Moodle. New Moodle installations have the module turned off by default. Assignments and blogs are taking the journal's place in Moodle.

- Finally, each journal is private, between the student and teacher only. This doesn't matter if you want the big idea writing to be private. But if you want the class to collaborate on this, or just to be able to see each other's writing, then journals won't work for you.

So, Why not a Blog?

In Moodle, each student can have a blog. This is turned on by default. However, a student's blog is not attached to any course. That is, you do not access a Moodle blog by going into a course and selecting the blog. Instead, you view the user's profile, and access that user's blog from there. In a Moodle student's blog, there is no way to associate a post with a course that the student is taking. This results in "blogging outside of the course". Also, as of version 1.9, you cannot leave comments on Moodle blogs.

If you tell your students to blog on their understanding of the big idea, you will need to visit each of your students' blogs to determine if they completed the assignment, and, you'll need to use some other way to give them a feedback on their writing. For these reasons, a Moodle blog is probably not the best way to have students relate new material to big ideas.

An Assignment

In newer versions of Moodle, the online text assignment is intended to replace the journal activity. It also shares the journal's disadvantages of not saving a history of the student's edits, and of forcing you to make the activity individual. However, an assignment does enable you to use any one of Moodle's standard or custom grading scales, to grade the student's assignment, and to leave a written feedback.

Let's Agree to Disagree

We have examined five activities for making big ideas, a part of our course. While you might disagree with my conclusion (I assume about four-fifths of my readers will), I'm glad that you stuck with the arguments this far. If you have reached a different conclusion, I know that you did so in a logical, informed way. The table that's coming up, compares each of the options we looked at:

Activity	Saves History	Enables Grading	Enables Feedback	Enables Collaboration	Individual Activity	Exists within Course
Assignment	No	Yes	Yes	No	Yes	Yes
Blog	Yes	No	No	No	Yes	No
Forum	Yes	Yes	Yes	Yes	Yes	Yes
Journal	No	Yes	Yes	No	Yes	Yes
Wiki	Yes	No	Yes	Yes	Yes	Yes

There is no perfect option here. I could also have suggested that you use an online text assignment after each topic, and require the student to relate material learned in that topic to the big ideas of the course. At the end of the course, you could require the student to copy and paste all of the topic assignments into one last assignment, and revise them into a final big idea submission. There is much discussion about the appropriate and creative uses of these activities on the www.moodle.org forums.

Individual Student Wikis

We usually think of a wiki as a group activity. However, Moodle enables you to create an individual wiki for each student enrolled in your course. Every student gets his/her own wiki, which only you and the student can edit. Like any other activity, you can choose whether to allow other students and groups to see each other's wikis.

This doesn't mean that you must create each student's wiki one at a time. Instead, you could create a wiki as you normally would, and designate it as a "Student Wiki". The first time that any student accesses the wiki, Moodle creates that student's personal wiki.

Individual student wikis can be used for several teaching strategies. In this section, we'll explore two of them: one-on-one instruction, and guided note taking.

Chapter 1 discusses some of the advantages of using Socratic dialogue as a teaching strategy. In a traditional classroom, Socratic dialogue is a discussion between the teacher and students. It requires one-to-one communication between the student and teacher. Online, you can hold one-to-one discussions with your students by giving each of them an individual wiki. If you set the **Group mode** to **No**, your discussions can be kept private.

Using a wiki for these discussions, enables students to review and edit previous posts as their understanding changes. It also puts all the discussion in one place, unlike using a series of email messages or forum postings.

Creating Individual Wikis

This book assumes some proficiency with Moodle, so I won't give click-by-click directions for creating a wiki. The key to creating an individual wiki for each student is the **Type** setting on the **Editing Wiki** page. From the **Type** drop-down menu, select **Student**. This is shown as follows:

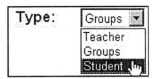

Each time a new student accesses the wiki from the course home page, an individual wiki will be created for that student. The second and subsequent times a student accesses the wiki, (s)he is taken to that student's personal wiki.

Guided Note Taking with Individual Student Wikis

Chapter 1 discusses some of the advantages of using guided notes. In a traditional classroom, you might copy a high-level outline for the course and distribute it to the students. They could use this as a guide for taking notes. In an online course, you can create a wiki for each student to populate with course notes. This wiki can have starting pages, which provide a guide for the student to enter notes. In this section, we'll see how to create an individual wiki for each student in a course, and how to pre-populate that wiki with starting pages that you create. This gives each student a place for guided note taking.

Detailed directions are in the subsections that follow. The overall process follows this order:

1. **Create the Wiki's Starting Pages**: Create a text file for the wiki's homepage. If desired, create additional text files for additional starting pages. Upload text files to the course.

2. **Create the Individual Student Wiki**: Create an individual, student wiki in your course. While creating the wiki, select the text files for the initial pages. Test the wiki as a student.

Creating a Text File for the Wiki's Starting Page

For every starting page that you want your wiki to have, you must create and upload a text file. In order to create the wiki, you must select the text file(s). Later, we will deal with uploading and selecting the text files. First, we must deal with creating the text files for our wiki's starting pages.

Text files use Wiki Markup for formatting commands. The purpose of these commands is to enable an author to quickly format text, while typing, without going to a menu. For example, to create a small headline (the equivalent of a Heading 3 in Word or your HTML editor), you would type `!Headline`. This would create a heading that looks like this:

> **Headline**

To create a medium headline (Heading 2), use two exclamation marks. For a large headline (Heading 1), use three. For example, `!!Heading` would look like this:

> **Headline**

If you want the starting page of your wiki to contain the first-level headings for an outline, you might create a text file called **Microscopy** that contains this text:

```
!!!Microscopy and Specimen Preparation

[Lenses and the Bending of Light | Lenses_and_the_Bending_of_Light]

[The Light Microscope |The_Light_Microscope]

[Preparation and Staining of Specimens | Preparation_and_Staining_
of_Specimens]
```

If you chose that text file as the starting page for a wiki, the first time a student accessed the wiki (s)he would see this:

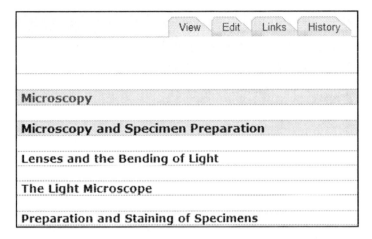

Note that the name of the text file, Microscopy, became the name of the page. Also note that the text preceded by !!! became a top level heading. And, the text inside square brackets became links.

At this page, the student would then select the **Edit** link and begin filling in this outline.

Building on our example from above, you can enter second level headings on the same page. The file Microscopy.txt would contain this:

```
!!!Microscopy and Specimen Preparation

!!Lenses and the Bending of Light

!Refraction

!Focal Point

!!The Light Microscope
```

```
!The Bright-field Microscope

!Resolution

!The Dark-field Microscope

!!Preparation and Staining of Specimens

!Fixation

!Dyes and Simple Staining

!Differential Staining
```

When that text file is uploaded and made a starting page for the wiki, the resulting starting page would look like this:

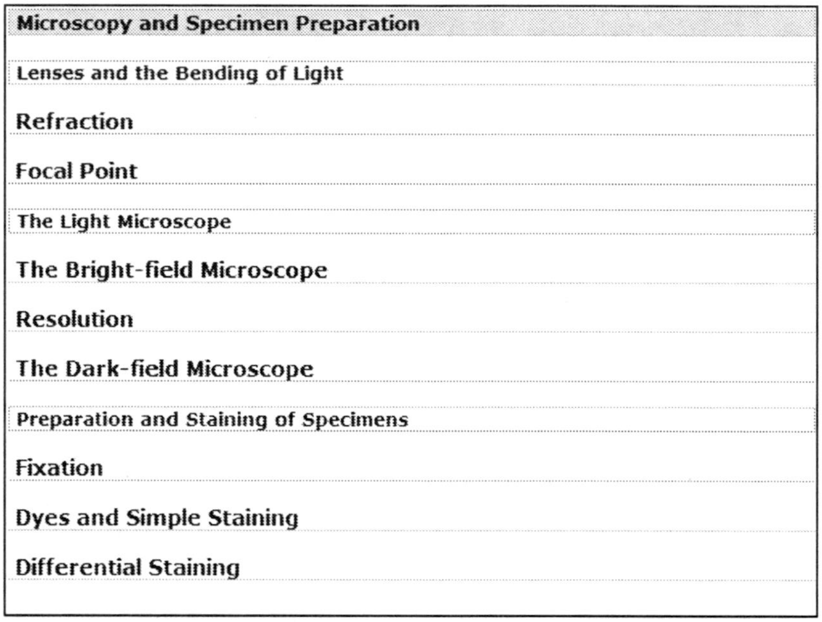

Microscopy and Specimen Preparation
Lenses and the Bending of Light
Refraction
Focal Point
The Light Microscope
The Bright-field Microscope
Resolution
The Dark-field Microscope
Preparation and Staining of Specimens
Fixation
Dyes and Simple Staining
Differential Staining

If you leave this page as it is, the student might put all of his or her notes for these topics on this one page. If you want to guide the student into using separate pages for each of these topics, you will need to create a separate page for each topic. You can put links to the topic pages from this starting page. It is the same idea as creating a home page, and providing links to the inside pages of a website.

Creating Multiple Starting Pages

In the section above, you saw how to create a single starting page for a wiki. You can also create multiple starting pages for a wiki. And, you can link to those pages from the wiki's home page.

Moodle enables you to create multiple starting pages for a wiki. In our example, we want to create four pages for our wiki:

- The starting page
- Lenses and the Bending of Light
- The Light Microscope
- Preparation and Staining of Specimens

On the starting page, we want links to the other three pages. The resulting wiki home-page would look like this:

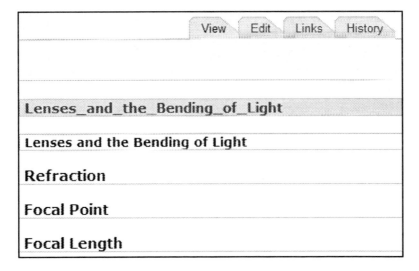

If a student followed the link to the page **Lenses and the Bending of Light**, (s)he would see the following:

First, let's discuss how to create multiple starting pages. Then, we'll discuss how to create links to the starting pages from the wiki's home-page.

Multiple Text Files Create Multiple Starting Pages

So, we need to create and upload a text file for each starting page in our wiki. In our example, the text files for the starting page and the three topic pages would look like this:

Microscopy.txt

```
!!!Microscopy and Specimen Preparation

[Lenses and the Bending of Light | Lenses_and_the_Bending_of_Light]

[The Light Microscope | The_Light_Microscope]

[Preparation and Staining of Specimens | Preparation_and_Staining_of_
Specimens]
```

Lenses_and_the_Bending_of_Light.txt

```
!!Lenses and the Bending of Light

!Refraction

!Focal Point
```

The_Light_Microscope.txt

```
!!The Light Microscope

!The Bright-field Microscope

!Resolution

!The Dark-field Microscope
```

Preparation_and_Staining_of_Specimens.txt

```
!!Preparation and Staining of Specimens

!Fixation

!Dyes and Simple Staining

!Differential Staining
```

Creating Links to Other Starting Pages

The file Microscopy.txt will have links to the other three pages. In the Wiki Markup language, links are encased in square brackets, like this: [The_Light_ Microscope] where, "The_Light_Microscope" is the name of the page in the wiki. By default, the link displays the name of the page. If you want the link to display something other than the name of the page, such as "Light Microscopes" you can add that to the markup:

```
[Light Microscopes | The_Light_Microscope]
```

This creates a link that displays **Light Microscopes** and takes the reader to a page called **The_Light_Microscope**.

In the links, notice the page names have underscores in them. Remember that the first part, Light Microscopes, is what the link will display. The second part, The_Light_Microscope, is the page that the link jumps to.

"Why the underscores?" These underscores are to accommodate a quirk that Moodle has. When Moodle uploads the text files that create these pages, it adds underscores to their names. For example, if you upload a file called The Light Microscope.txt, Moodle changes its name to The_Light_Microscope.txt. Since the wiki pages are named after the text files that you upload, the wiki pages will also have underscores in their names. Therefore, the links to the starting pages created from those text files need the underscores.

After you've created a text file for each starting page that you want in your wiki, you are ready to upload them.

Upload the Text Files for the Wiki's Starting Pages to Your Course

On your course's home-page, from the Administration block, select the files you want to upload.

In the resulting window, click on the **Create New Folder** (📁) button and use a similar name as the one in the wiki, to name it.

Upload the text files to the folder. As this book assumes some proficiency with Moodle, I won't give you click-by-click directions for uploading the files. But the result will look like this:

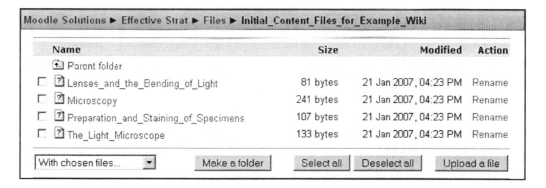

Note in the example above, that after the files were uploaded, Moodle added underscores to the file names. The file that started out as The Light Microscope.txt, became The_Light_Microscope.txt. The wiki starting page created from this text file will also have underscores in its name, thus it will be **The_Light_Microscope**.

Also notice in the example above that the navigation bar (the "breadcrumbs" at the top of the page) shows us the course name, then **Files**, and then the name of the folder we created for our text files.

Create an Individual Student Wiki in your Course

Once again, this book assumes some proficiency with Moodle. So I won't give you click-by-click directions for creating a wiki. The key is that while creating the wiki, from the **Type** drop-down menu, select **Student**. This is shown in the following screenshot:

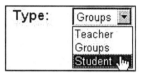

Now each time a new student accesses the wiki from the course home page, an individual wiki will be created for that student. The second and subsequent times a student accesses the wiki, (s)he is taken to that student's personal wiki.

The **HTML Mode** setting will affect how your starting page looks. In the following example, I've selected **No HTML** because I am using Wiki Markup language in the text files:

If I select one of the HTML modes, the starting page will not display properly because the text file doesn't contain valid HTML; it contains wiki markup instead.

Skipping ahead to the end result, this is what I would get by selecting an HTML mode instead of Wiki Markup:

You can see that the line breaks between the links were lost. If you want to use HTML in your wiki, the text files that create your initial pages must be written with HTML. If you want to use Wiki Markup language, the text files must be written in Wiki Markup language.

While Creating the Wiki, Select the Text Files for the Initial Pages

While creating the wiki, under **Choose an Initial Page**, click the **Choose/upload initial page** button and navigate to the folder where you stored the text files. This folder should contain *only* the text files for the starting pages.

From within the folder, select the text file for the starting page that will become the home page of the wiki. Any other text file in that folder will become an additional page. In the following screenshot, **Microscopy** becomes the home page for the wiki, and the other text files become additional starting pages.

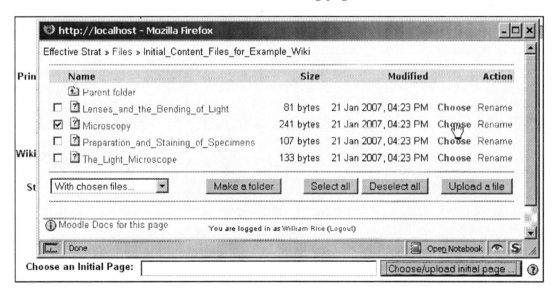

Notice that I needed to select only **Microscopy**. The other files in this directory, automatically become starting pages. That is why it is important that this directory contains only text files for the starting pages in your wiki.

Test the Wiki as a Student

When creating a course, it is helpful to keep two separate browsers running, such as Internet Explorer and Firefox. In one browser, create the course. In the other, log in as a student, and test as you create.

The result of uploading these text files, and choosing **Microscopy** as the starting page, looks like this:

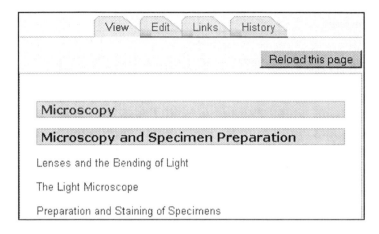

If we select the site map for the wiki, you can see the organization of the starting pages, in the following screenshot:

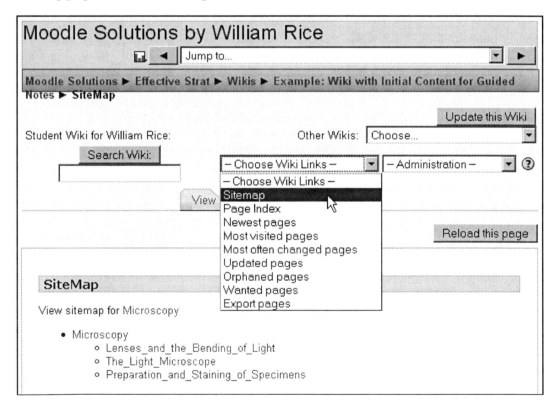

Once a student has viewed the wiki, you can no longer change the starting page(s). At that point, if you want a wiki with different starting pages, you must create a new wiki.

Leveraging Guided Notes Created by Students

In the business world, to "leverage" something, is to take maximum advantage of it. You can leverage the guided notes created by your students. First, the students' notes tell you what the students thought you wanted them to learn, and what they considered important. This might be very different from what you actually wanted them to learn, and from what you considered important. Imagine you're giving your students a test and discovering that the entire class has learned some very different material from what you included in the test. Reviewing the students' guided notes periodically, can avoid this kind of surprise, and give you an insight into their progress. This is something we can't do when the students take notes on paper.

Suggested Wiki Etiquettes

No wiki software offers every feature. Each wiki application offers its own blend of features. Some points of wiki etiquettes apply only to certain features and others only to certain environments. With Moodle's wiki features and the e-learning environment in mind, I will offer some suggested etiquettes for your Moodle wikis.

You can download these rules as a file from the publisher's website, www.packtpub. com. Feel free to modify and distribute them for use in all your Moodle courses.

- **Just do it**: Nike's slogan could also apply to wikis. Add a paragraph, correct some grammar or some spelling, fix a broken link, create a new page, etc. A wiki is a collaboration, so jump in and collaborate.

- **Help to organize and create structure**: Even if you're not creating new content, you can organize the already existing content. Give your pages names that help users identify them. Create cross-links between pages. When you find content on a page that belongs to a different page, cut and paste it. Making information easy to find, is just as important as creating it.

- **Comment thoughtfully**: A wiki is not instant messaging. It's not meant to be a high-speed conversation. And while a wiki is not the most formal type of writing, it is not entirely informal. Even if what you write is deleted, it will remain in the wiki's history. Express your opinions carefully.

- **Add items to lists**: If someone has created a list of items, feel free to add to it. But please add the items in alphabetical or logical order.

- **Be polite**: Just as with chats, it's easy to misinterpret the tone of a comment. So, please be polite.

- **Don't write "click here"**: Instead, create links that describe what the reader will see when they follow the link.

- **Avoid creating blank pages**: Remember that when you insert a link into a wiki (using Camel Case or the square brackets), a page is created when you click on the link, and not otherwise. Unless you have content to add, don't click on a link that creates a new page. All pages show up in the Sitemap, including blank pages. A sitemap full of blank pages can mislead and disappoint the reader. If you have some content for the page, by all means, create it. If not, leave the link untouched.

- **Preserve the meaning**: *The meaning of something can change with its context.* When you move or delete material, make sure that you are not unintentionally changing the meaning of the remaining material.

- **Chill! Don't take it personally**: Your work will be edited, and you will not agree with every change. That's the nature of collaboration.

- **Delete carefully**: If you can achieve your goal by adding to or editing an entry, do that instead of deleting it. Most contributors have reasons for adding an entry. They might feel their time has been wasted if they see their entries being deleted.

- **Discuss things elsewhere**: Moodle enables you to see who has edited an entry. If you want to discuss an entry with its authors, use means such as email, chat, forum, etc. The wiki is the place to *produce* content, not to discuss it.

Summary

In this chapter, we saw how to use a wiki for relating material to a big idea, one-on-one discussion, and guided note taking. The section on big idea wikis compared Moodle's `Wiki` module to its `Assignment`, `Blog`, `Forum`, and `Journal` modules. You may have noticed that in Moodle, these modules are missing some elements that you would expect, but include some elements that surprised you. This is because each of Module's capabilities and limitations are chosen so that it supports online learning and fits into Moodle's environment. For example, Moodle blogs do not allow readers to comment. This is because the developers and community are still discussing whether blog comments will pull valuable discussion out of a course and into a student's blog (recall that a blog belongs to a user, not to a course). To find out more about the rationale behind decisions like this, and to compare capabilities of the various module's, read the `www.moodle.org` forums.

The ability to create individual student wikis is one of Moodle's surprising, and often under used capabilities. The same can be said for creating starting pages in a wiki. Whenever you need to guide a student's writing, consider an individual wiki with starting pages. You can also find other creative uses of Moodle wikis.

7
Glossary Solutions

Most people think of glossaries as nothing more than special-purpose, online dictionaries. But, a glossary can also be an enjoyable, collaborative activity for your class, and a teaching tool. Let's look at the capabilities of the Glossary module first, and then ideas for using glossaries for more than just vocabulary building.

Moodle's Glossary Functions

As this book assumes basic proficiency with Moodle, we won't cover click-by-click directions for creating and using glossaries. However, we will review some of the capabilities of a glossary. Then, we'll see how we can make creative use of these capabilities.

Automatic Linking to a Glossary

Moodle can automatically link a term, wherever it appears in a course, to the term's glossary entry. Note that three things must be set for this to happen:

1. The glossary must be in the same course as the term or the glossary must be available throughout the site (see the topic *Course versus Site Glossary* that's coming up next).

2. The term must match the name of the glossary entry or one of the entry's aliases.

3. Automatic linking must be turned ON for the glossary and glossary entry.

Course versus Site Glossary

When you create a glossary, it is added to the course in which you created it. If you have administrator privileges on your Moodle site, you can make a glossary global, which makes it active for every course on your site.

Main versus Secondary Glossary

Each course can have only one main glossary. It can have many secondary glossaries. The content of each secondary glossary shows up in the main glossary. This would enable easy and clear-cut segregation of the contents in the main glossary.

Managing Student Contributions to a Glossary

You can allow students to contribute to a glossary. Several features help you to manage this process.

By default, students can add new entries to a glossary. If you want to turn this OFF, you won't find it with the rest of the settings on the **Editing Glossary** page. Instead, you'll need to go to the **Roles** tab of the **Editing Glossary** page, select the **Override roles** sub tab, then select the **Student** role, and take away this permission.

By default, **Duplicate entries allowed** is set to **No**. If you are allowing student contributions to a glossary, you might want to set this to **Yes**. If you forbid duplicates, you might want to assign your students to specific entries so that they do not try to create duplicates. You might also want to set **Allow comments on entries** to **Yes**, so that if a student can't create the entry (s)he wanted to, the student can still comment on it.

Approved by default determines if an entry created by a student is added to the glossary without the teacher's approval. If you've assigned each student specific glossary entries, you might want to set this to **No**. Then, when a student creates the assigned glossary entries, they appear under the **Waiting approval** tab of the glossary. This gives you a convenient place to check whether the student has completed the assignment. If you set this to **Yes**, then entries created by students go right into the glossary, and you need to search the entire glossary to determine if a student has completed the assigned entries.

Edit always allows you to decide if students can edit their entries at any time. If you set this to **Yes**, a student can always return to the entries (s)he created and edit them. If you set this to **No**, a student cannot edit his/her entries after the editing time has passed. The editing time for a glossary is the same as for a forum posting. By default, Moodle gives a contributor 30 minutes to edit a glossary entry or forum posting before it is added. You can set this under site administration.

Ratings and Comments

You can give students the ability to rate glossary entries, just like they can rate forum postings. The question is, what do you want the students to rate:

- The clarity of the glossary entry
- Its helpfulness
- Your writing skill, in creating the entry.

You'll need to consider what you want students to rate, and create a custom scale that supports the rating. You determine who can rate glossary entries, and what scale to use, on the **Editing Glossary** page:

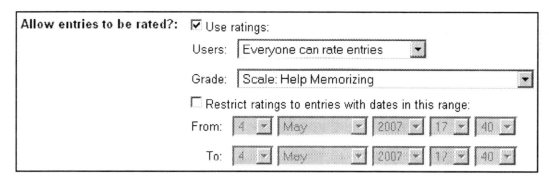

You must have read about creating a custom scale in the subsection *Use a Custom Scale to Rate Relevance* in *Chapter 2: Forum Solutions*. Creating and applying a custom scale to glossary entries is the same as creating and applying it to forum entries.

Adding Memory Aids to Glossary Entries

Some subjects require memorization. This is an unpleasant fact of teaching, and learning. Vocabulary, formulae, and classifications, all require students to memorize. Reminders and mnemonics are memory aids that can make memorizing faster and easier for your students.

One way to include memory aids in your course is to add them to glossary entries, as shown in the following example:

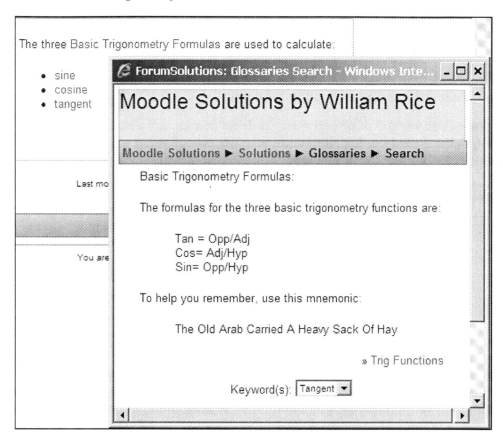

If you add memory aids to your glossary entries, consider giving the students a scale to rate the usefulness of each memory aid. You'll need to give the students directions on how to use the scale. Note that in the previous screenshot that the scale is not displayed with the entry. The student needs to click on **Trig Functions** to enter the glossary, and then, if you have enabled ratings and/or comments, the student can rate, and comment on the entry:

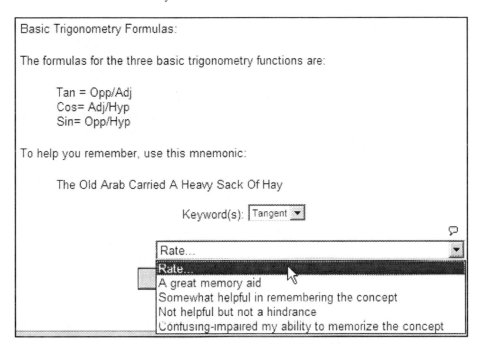

To leave a comment on this entry, the student clicks on 🗩 and types a comment into the editing window. The comment is not displayed with the glossary entry. To see an entry's comments, you must enter into the glossary, as the student has done in the previous screenshot.

Student-Created Class Directory

You can use a glossary for your class directory. Instruct the student to create a glossary entry for themselves. There are several things you can do to make this exercise easier for the students:

- First, create a web page that the students can use as a template with placeholders for the information you want them to include. Also, on this page, state the limitations for how personal the information will be.

- Tell the students if this glossary will be global or visible only to the class. They should know if you intend to reveal information about them to all of the other people who use your site.

- Consider leaving the **Edit always** function set to **Yes**. If a student wants to update his/her entry, or has second thoughts about some information (s)he included, the student should be able to easily edit the entry.

- If you ask students to include a picture in their glossary entry, give them directions for uploading and including pictures on a page. Although, including a picture on a web page in Moodle is quite simple, and similar to the way it's done in most blogging sites, include the directions anyway.

- You probably would want to turn off auto-linking for this glossary. If a student has the same name as another person who is studying in the course, or adds keywords that show up in the course, you would want a link to that student's glossary-biography to appear in the course.

If you assign this early in the course, students will gain practice with Moodle's online editor. The editor is the same for a glossary entry, web page, or text assignment, so this practice can be very useful.

Moodle comes with a **Random Glossary Entry** block, as shown in the next screenshot. You can add this block to your course, and set it to display a new student from the directory (the glossary) every day. There is more about random glossaries in the last section of this chapter.

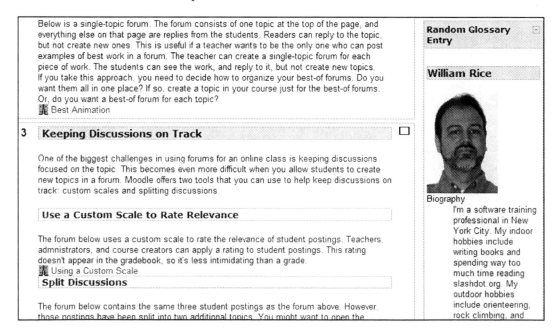

Student-Created Test Questions

You can use a glossary to collect test questions from your students. Have them create test questions based on the work that they've done in class, and submit each question as a glossary entry.

Set **Approve by default** to **No**, unless you want students to see the questions that their classmates submit. Also, turn off automatic linking for the test question glossary.

After your students have submitted enough questions, you can pick the best entries for an exam.

Making Use of the Random Glossary Block

Moodle's **Random Glossary Block** pulls entries from a selected glossary, and displays them in a block. It can pull entries from any glossary that is available in that course.

Even though the name is *Random Glossary Block*, you can control the order in which entries are pulled from the glossary, and how often the block displays a new entry. For example, in the screenshot that's coming up, the **Random Glossary Block** is set to display each entry in order, and to change each day:

Configuring a Random Glossary Entry block	
Title:	Quotable Number Crunchers
Take entries from this glossary:	Famous Math Quotes ▾
Days before a new entry is chosen:	1
How a new entry is chosen:	Next entry ▾ ⑦
Show concept (heading) for each entry:	☑
You can display links to actions of the glossary this block is associated with. The block will only display links to actions which are enabled for that glossary.	
When users can add entries to the glossary, show a link with this text:	Add a favorite quotation.
When users can view the glossary but not add entries, show a link with this text:	More quotations...
When users cannot edit or view the glossary, show this text (without link):	Check back tomorrow for another quote.
	Save changes

Here are some ideas for using the **Random Glossary Block** for something other than a glossary:

- **Highlights** from work that past students in a class submitted. If a class is working on a long-term project, create a glossary that contains the best work submitted by the past students who have completed working on it. Display the glossary while the current class is working on that project.

- Inspirational or informative **quotes** related to the field of study.

- If you're teaching in a corporate setting, consider putting **rules and procedures** into their own glossaries. You could create a separate glossary for each type of rule or procedure. For example, a Human Resources Policies glossary, a Purchase Order glossary, etc. Then, display random entries from these glossaries in the appropriate courses.

- Create a glossary with **past exam questions** and their answers. Students can use this as another resource to prepare for exams.

- Funny **anecdotes** related to the field of study.

- **Common mistakes** and their corrections. For example, how to spot software bugs, or common foreign language grammar errors.

Summary

In this chapter, we studied about how a glossary can be useful in the Moodle environment. To make a good Moodle glossary, think beyond using it just for vocabulary. A collection of brief material such as quotes, tips, short stories, rules, policies, examples, frequently asked questions, etc. can be made into a glossary. If you're going to create a web page with a list of items, ask yourself if you could use a glossary instead.

The big advantage a glossary holds over a simple web page, is its constant presence in the sidebar. With the **Random Glossary Block**, you can put new information in front of the student every time (s)he logs into your course. The student doesn't need to click into a web page to see that information. Also, you can allow students to contribute to the glossary, which makes it an interactive activity.

The Choice Activity

8

Moodle's Choice is the simplest type of activity. In this activity, you create one question, and specify a choice of responses. You can use a choice to:

- Take a quick poll.
- Ask students to choose sides in a debate.
- Confirm the students' understanding of an agreement.
- Gather consent.

Before we look at how to accomplish this, let's look at the Choice activity from the student's point of view, and then explore the settings available to the teacher while creating a Choice.

A Look at the Choice Activity

Before we discuss some of the uses of a Choice activity, let's look at a *choice* from both the students' and teachers' point of view.

Students' Point of View

From the students' point of view, a Choice activity looks like this:

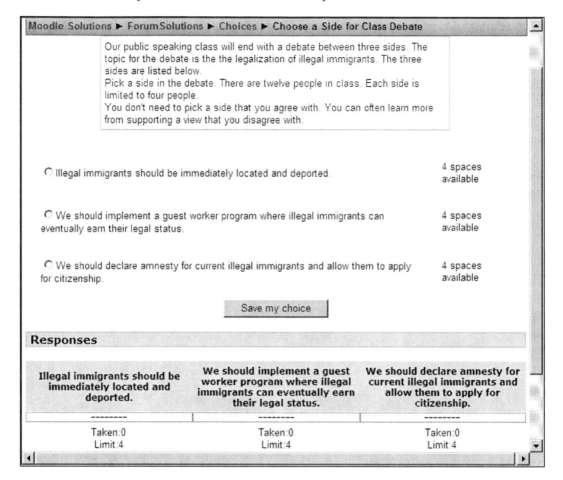

Note that at the bottom of the window, the student can see how many other students have chosen a response. There is also a limit on the number of students who can choose each response.

Teachers' Point of View

Before we discuss some of the uses of a Choice activity, let's look at the settings available on the **Editing Choice** page. Then, we'll see how we can make creative use of these capabilities.

Number of Choices

When you first use the **Editing Choice** page, Moodle gives you space for five responses:

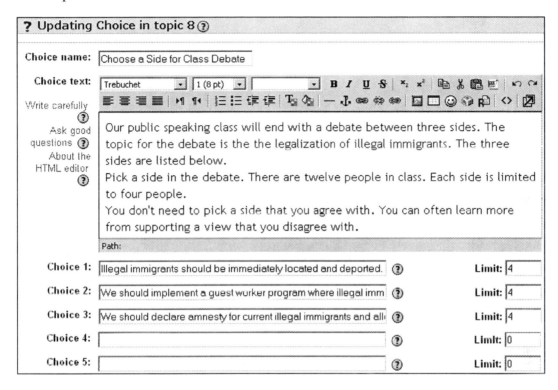

If you have used up all the choices, and need more choices, save the activity and exit. When you return to the editing page, Moodle gives you two more blank choices. You can continue doing this until Moodle has created as many choices as you need.

Limit

The **Limit** next to each choice enables you to limit how many students can select that choice. In the example above, no more than four students can select each choice. So after four students have selected **Choice 1**, that choice becomes unavailable. Limits must be enabled for the choice by clicking on **Enable** as shown in the following screenshot:

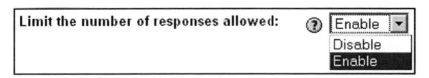

Time Limit

You can define a time period during which students are allowed to make a choice. If you don't set a time limit (if you leave the box unchecked), the choice is always available. The following screenshot shows you how to set the time limit:

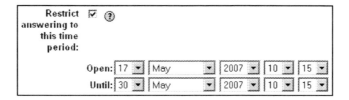

Publish Results

You can choose whether to reveal the results of the choice to the students, or not, by choosing an option from the drop-down menu, as shown in the following screenshot:

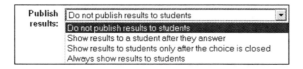

In the example at the beginning of this section, **Publish results** was set to **Always show results to students**. That is why the student could see how many students had chosen each response. If it had been set to **Do not publish results to students**, the activity would not have shown the number of students who selected each response. Note that at the bottom of the following screenshot, the number **Taken** and **Limit** are no longer displayed:

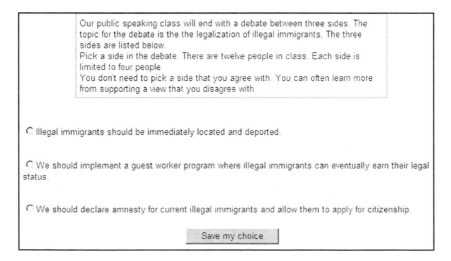

If you are going to limit the number of students, who can choose a response, consider using **Always show results to students**. That way, the student can see how many people have chosen the response, and how many slots are left for each response.

Privacy

If you publish the results of the choice, you can then choose whether to publish the names of the students who have selected each response:

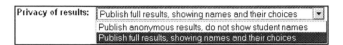

In the example at the beginning of this section, **Privacy of results** was set to **Publish anonymous results, do not show student names**. If it had been set to **Publish full results, showing names and their choices**, the student would have seen who had selected each response:

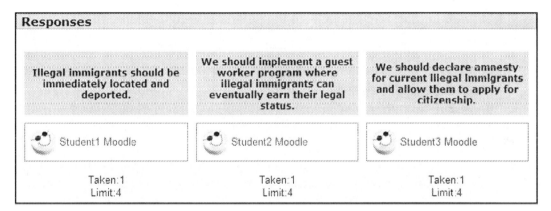

Allow Students to Change their Minds

The **Allow choice to be updated** setting, determines if a student can change his/her answer after submitting it. If this is set to **Yes**, a student can retake the choice activity until the activity is closed.

Choosing Teams

You can use a Choice activity to have students organize themselves into teams, as in the example that we've been using:

> Our public speaking class will end with a debate between three sides. The topic for the debate is the the legalization of illegal immigrants. The three sides are listed below.
> Pick a side in the debate. There are twelve people in class. Each side is limited to four people.
> You don't need to pick a side that you agree with. You can often learn more from supporting a view that you disagree with.
>
> ○ Illegal immigrants should be immediately located and deported.
>
> ○ We should implement a guest worker program where illegal immigrants can eventually earn their legal status.
>
> ○ We should declare amnesty for current illegal immigrants and allow them to apply for citizenship.

If you use a choice for this, there are some settings that will help your students. These are as follows:

- Firstly, you might want to use the **Limit** setting to set a limit on the number of students who choose each team. This ensures that each team contains the same number of students.

- Secondly, you will probably want to set a time limit on the activity. Instruct the students that, if they don't choose a side within the given time, you will assign them one.

- Finally, you may want to publish the results to the students. If you select **Always show results to students**, the students will be able to see if any team is short on members. By turning on the **Allow choice to be updated** setting, you can give the students the ability to spontaneously organize themselves into teams of approximately equal size.

Under **Privacy of results**, you can choose to show the students' names and results, if you don't mind them choosing teams based on friendship and compatibility. If learning to work with people who they might not like is one of your learning goals, you might want to publish the results anonymously instead.

Asking for Students' Consent

You can use a Choice activity to confirm the students' understanding of an agreement or record their consent. For example, if you're teaching a filmmaking class, and you anticipate entering the resulting film into student competitions, you could use a choice to record the students' consent to have their work submitted to the competition. Or, you could write the course syllabus and schedule as the text of the choice, and have the student confirm that (s)he has read the syllabus. This is shown in the following screenshot:

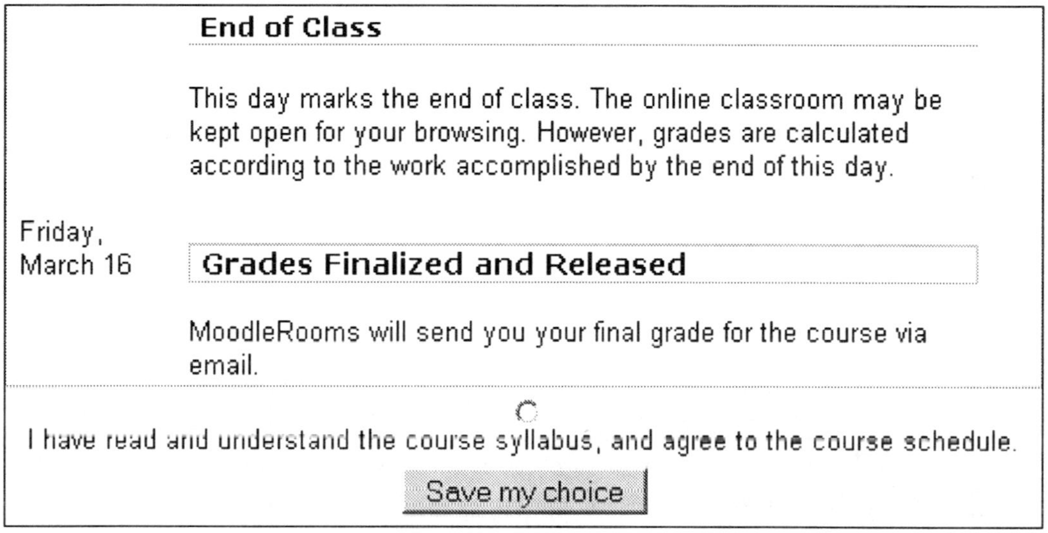

End of Class

This day marks the end of class. The online classroom may be kept open for your browsing. However, grades are calculated according to the work accomplished by the end of this day.

Friday, March 16

Grades Finalized and Released

MoodleRooms will send you your final grade for the course via email.

I have read and understand the course syllabus, and agree to the course schedule.

Save my choice

In this case, you might want the choice to have only one response, indicating the student's agreement. If you have a response indicating the student's disagreement, enable them to change their response, and decide how you will handle the disagreement.

You can also use a choice to survey the class about their readiness to proceed with an activity. This is especially useful if the class needs to coordinate their efforts. For example, if you're using one of Moodle's workshop activities, you can have students assess each other's work as part of their grade. If some students don't submit their work on time, this can hold up the entire activity. To ensure students understand the workshop and are ready to start, you can use a survey to quickly poll them. When the entire class has responded they are ready, you can proceed with the activity.

How are We Doing?

Consider creating a variety of choices to ask students about the pace, direction, and progress of your course. You can hide or reveal them whenever you want to poll the students. Place this kind of poll at the top of the page, under a heading to draw attention to it, as shown in the following screenshot:

Topic outline

Tuesday's Assignment Postponed Until Thursday

Due to the Memorial Day holiday, which the instructor did not account for when writing the syllabus, we have moved Tuesday's assignment to Thursday. Please download the updated syllabus, as some other dates have also changed.

Complete this Poll: Pace of the Course

Is the course moving too quickly for you? Not fast enough? Is it just right, and you want to maintain this pace for the duration? Speak up by taking this one-question poll. Please complete it now.

? Pace of the Course: click here!
News forum
Participants

Preview the Final

Since, a Choice activity is not an official "quiz", it can provide a non-threatening way to check the students' understanding of key concepts. Try preparing a variety of Choice activities with questions about the most difficult concepts in a lesson, and using them to take quick measurements of how well the students are assimilating the material. Or, create a series of choices called "Final Exam Questions". Tell the students that each of these questions will appear in the final exam, in a slightly different form, and that each will have a time limit. When the student reads the newest question, (s)he is rewarded with the answer to the previous question.

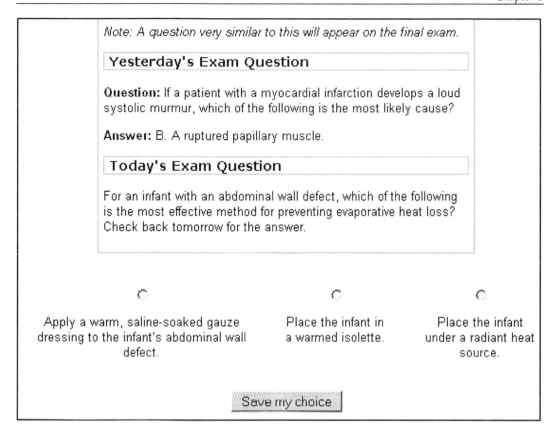

Note: A question very similar to this will appear on the final exam.

Yesterday's Exam Question

Question: If a patient with a myocardial infarction develops a loud systolic murmur, which of the following is the most likely cause?

Answer: B. A ruptured papillary muscle.

Today's Exam Question

For an infant with an abdominal wall defect, which of the following is the most effective method for preventing evaporative heat loss? Check back tomorrow for the answer.

Apply a warm, saline-soaked gauze dressing to the infant's abdominal wall defect.

Place the infant in a warmed isolette.

Place the infant under a radiant heat source.

Save my choice

This can motivate students to frequently check their progress in the course.

Summary

Moodle's Choice module is not only simple, but also very flexible. Its interface is less threatening than a Quiz, and its publishing features allow students to see the progress of a Choice, unlike a Survey. Whenever you need to gather a feedback, gain a consensus, or take a poll, consider using a Choice activity.

9
Course Solutions

By default, every course has a **Topic 0**, at the top of the course's home page. This topic is intended to hold information about the course. We usually begin adding the content of the course with Topic 1. For example, if a course uses a *Weekly* format, every topic will be assigned to one week, but Topic 0 will not have a date. If your course uses the *Topics* format, Topic 1 and onwards will be numbered, but Topic 0 will not be numbered. This indicates to the student that Topic 0 is not part of the course flow.

There are several kinds of information that fit well into Topic 0 of your course. In general, this is information that you want the student to see as soon as (s)he enters the course. Remember that the student won't see Topic 0 until after being enrolled, so don't include any information that the student might need before enrolling, such as the course description and prerequisites.

Am I in the Right Room?

If you've ever taught a class in person, you might have noticed that when students arrive for the first session they often look at the board and around the room for an indication that they have found the right room. Sometimes they even ask, "Is this the _____ class?". Online, students can have a similar experience.

Placing the course name and description at the very top of Topic 0 can give them the same reassurance as writing the course name on the board at the front of the room:

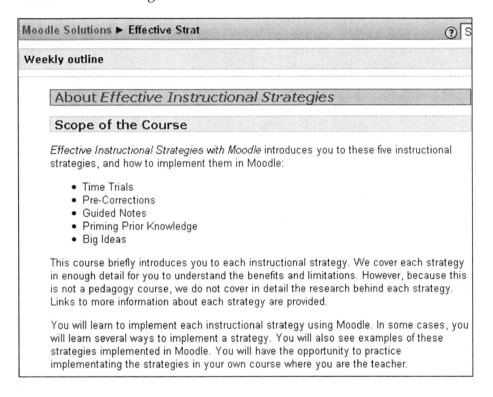

Important Announcements

By default, every course you create in Moodle is given a Topic 0 with a **News forum** added. The **Latest News** block is also automatically added. This block displays the latest announcement(s) added to the News Forum. In the next screenshot, you can see the result:

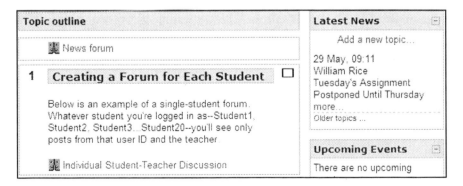

However, if the announcement is especially important, you might not want to count on your students to read the **Latest News** block. In these cases, consider using Topic 0 for critical announcements. Note the announcement in the next screenshot, and compare it with the previous screenshot:

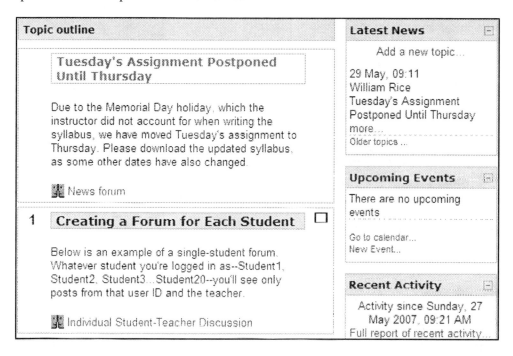

In this example, the teacher added a label to Topic 0. The headline was formatted with the style Heading 3 and made red. Then the label was positioned at the top of the topic.

Moving Blocks to the Main Course Area

The standard Moodle installation gives you the choice of two, one, or no side columns for your blocks. If you want to eliminate the side columns, you have more space for your course content, but no space for blocks. Let us explore a workaround for that. We'll use the **People** (also called **Participants**) block as an example.

Normally, the **People** block would occupy one of the side columns, which is a valuable screen space, and can be used for the main course content. This is as shown in the next screenshot:

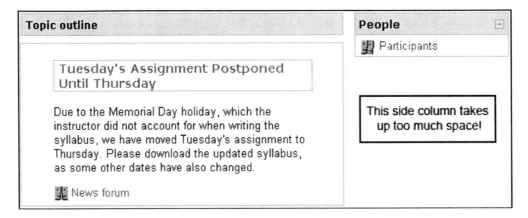

Now, what if we want to have the functionality of the block, without needing a side column? This is examined in the next section.

The Goal

We want to arrive at a solution that looks like this:

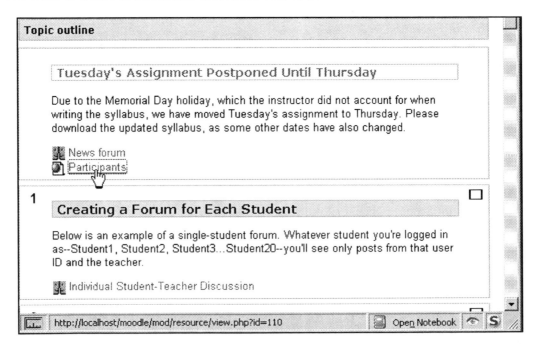

Note that instead of having a **People** block in one of the side columns, the course displays a link to the **Participants** in the main course area. There are no side columns, so the entire width of the page is given to course content.

You can see that in the following screenshot, the **Participants** link in the main course area, and in the **People** block, are the same:

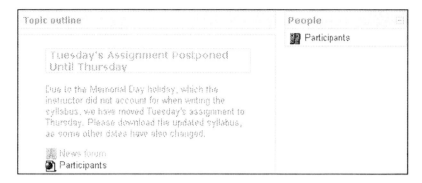

Comparing the Two Links

Both links go to the same URL. In this case, they both go to `http://localhost/moodle/user/index.php?contextid=71`, which is the list of participants.

So, clicking on either of these links takes you to the same place, that is, the list of the participants in this course:

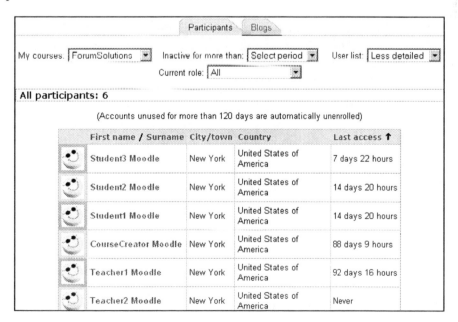

Even if the block is hidden, visiting this URL will display the list of participants. You don't need to display a block in your course to get it to work. You just need to visit the URL for that block. We use this to our advantage. If we copy the link(s) from a block, and paste it into the main course area, we can hide the block and possibly eliminate the side column for the block.

A Caveat

However, there is a significant difference between the links shown previously. The **Participants** link generated by the **People** block is dynamic. If this course is moved to another domain, or moved to another URL, or is backed up and then restored (copied) to another location, that link will be regenerated by the **People** block. It will work no matter where this course is moved or copied.

The **Participants** link in the main course area is not dynamic. I copied the URL from the **People** block and pasted it into the course. If the URL of the **Participants** block changes—because the course is moved to another domain, or moved to another URL, or is backed up and then restored to another location—this link will still point to the old location.

This method creates a static link in your course area. The link is not updated dynamically, like the links generated by a block. When you move a course, the link will break.

The Method

To create a link to the block, I started with the block displayed in the side column. Then I right-clicked on the link and copied it, as shown in the following screenshot:

Once I copied the link location, I created a new link in the main course area, as shown in the next screenshot:

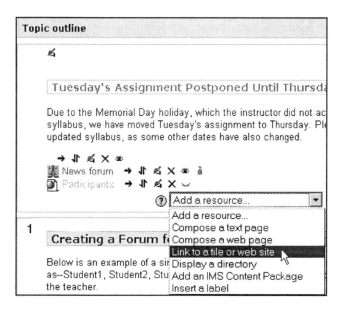

Then I hid the block, as you can see in the following screenshot of the editing mode. Note that the eye in the **People** block is closed:

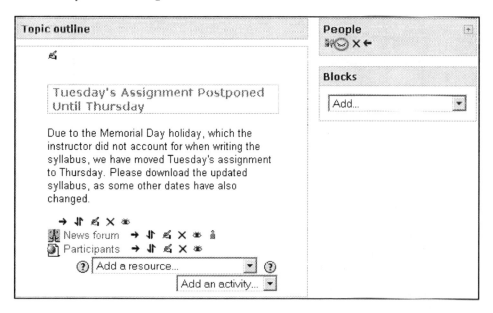

So, while the block does exist and has been added to this course, it is hidden from view. Therefore, it takes no space in the right column, and the entire page is given to the course's content.

Using this Workaround with Other Blocks

You can copy any link generated by a block, and paste it into the main area of your course. Then, you can hide the block, and eliminate the side column that would have held the block. However, you will need to experiment with each link to determine if it works.

Section Links

The **Section Links** block creates a link to each visible section in your course:

Note that the links are just numbers. They do not give you the title of each section. You can copy each of these links, and place them in Topic 0, and then, label each link. It would look like this:

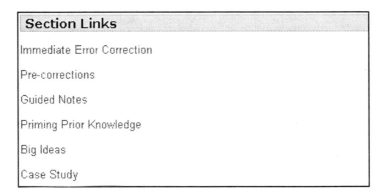

When using this method to create section links, you must remember two things:

- Firstly, as stated before, these links are static. They will not be updated if you move your course. If you are working on a development server, make these links for your production server.

- Secondly, while creating the link in Moodle, for the **Target** select **Same frame**.

Refer to the following screenshot:

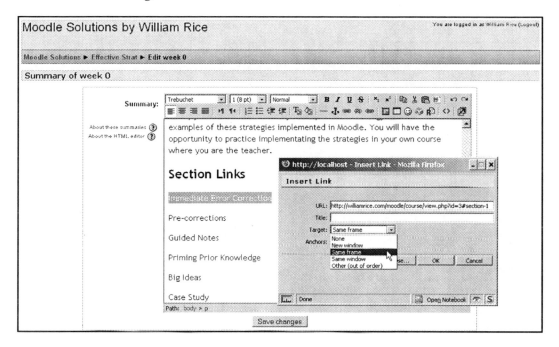

This makes the link open in the same window and frame. The effect is that the page scrolls down to the section.

Activities

The **Activities** block displays links to each kind of activity in your course, as shown in the following figure:

Clicking on any of these links displays all of the activities of that type in your course. For example, clicking on the **Assignments** link displays this:

Week	Name	Assignment type	Due date	Submitted	Grade
1	Example: Immediate Error Correction in an Assignment	Upload a single file	Tuesday, 6 February 2007, 05:00 PM	View 1 submitted assignments	-
	Practice: Create a Lesson with Remedial Information	Offline activity	Thursday, 8 February 2007, 05:00 PM	View 0 submitted assignments	-
2	Practice Part 1: Create a Workshop with Teacher Example	Offline activity	Tuesday, 13 February 2007, 05:00 PM	View 0 submitted assignments	-
	Pactice Part 2: Assess Another Student's Teacher Example	Offline activity	Thursday, 15 February 2007, 05:00 PM	View 0 submitted assignments	-
	Practice Part 3: Assess Your Student's Work	Offline activity	Friday, 16 February 2007, 05:00 PM	View 0 submitted assignments	-

If an activity type appears in your course, a link to that type appears in the block. If your course does not have a given type of activity, then a link to that type will not be displayed. For example, if your course does not have any assignments, then the **Assignments** link will not appear in the block. If you add an activity type to a course, then the block is dynamically updated with that type of activity.

You can copy the links from this block and place them in your main course area. Then you can hide the block and possibly eliminate the sidebar that it occupied. However, as noted before, the block is dynamically updated if you add a new type of activity to your course.

The Syllabus

Including a link to the course syllabus from Topic 0 is almost obvious. I suggest two refinements to your syllabus.

Printer-Friendly for Letter and A4 Sizes

First, make the syllabus printer-friendly. Even though we live in "the computer age", many people still prefer to have a hardcopy of their schedules and tasks. Providing the syllabus in .pdf format makes it easier for the student to generate a printout.

If you have students in both North America and the rest of the world, you will want the printout to be formatted so that it prints well on both Letter and A4 sized paper. Letter sized paper is shorter than A4, at 11 inches (279.4 mm). A4 sized paper is narrower than Letter, at 8.27 inches (210 mm). To ensure your printout will fit on either paper; consider using an A4 size page. Then, to ensure that content doesn't go outside the printable area, use margins of .5 inches to keep the material inside the printable area of the paper. This will take care of the top, left, and right margins for students who are using both A4 and Letter paper.

As A4 is .7 inch (18 mm) longer than Letter, use hard page breaks to give an additional .7 inch of space between the last line of your page and the margin. That will make the document print properly on Letter size paper. So the space between the last text on a page and the bottom of the page will be 1.2 inches, .5 inch margin and another .7 inch due to the hard page break.

Online Calendar with Event Reminders

Google, Yahoo!, 30boxes.com, and others offer online calendars that you can open to the public. These online calendars can be accessed with desktop calendars such as Outlook, iCal, Evolution, KOrganizer, and Sunbird. For example, students can access my course calendar on Google by subscribing via an XMLS feed, iCal subscription, or viewing an HTML page:

Calendar Address: XML ICAL HTML

Learn more
Change sharing settings

This is the address for your calendar. No one can use this link unless you have made your calendar public.

Most online calendars can send reminders of events via email. Sending a reminder of an assignment the day before it's due can be a good way to help your students stay on schedule. However, most online calendars can send reminders to only one email address. To send reminders to all of the students in the class, consider using an online group, such as a Google group or Yahoo! group. For example, here I am creating an event with a reminder in my Yahoo! group:

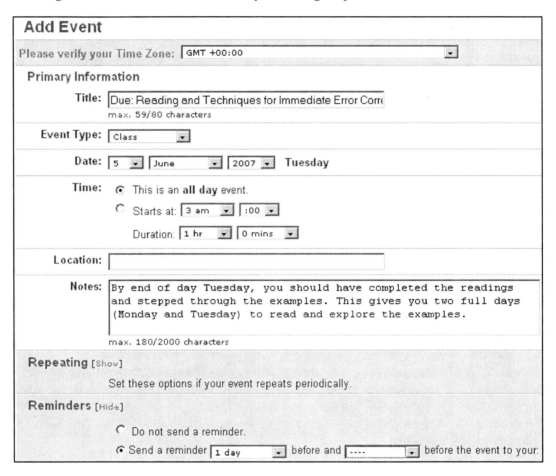

Note that the event is actually an assignment, which is due on that day. Refer to **Due: Reading and Techniques for Immediate Error Correction in the screenshot above.** Also notice that under the **Reminders** section, I'm sending an email reminder to everyone in the group one day before. Students, who choose to join this group will receive an email reminder for each assignment when it is due.

Summary

In this chapter, the solutions focused on making your course easier to navigate. The goal of all these solutions is to reduce the time and effort your students spend figuring out what to do next, so that they can get on with the learning. Topic 0 is useful for introductory information, and for keeping students up-to-date with current announcements. Moving blocks to the main course area eliminates the side bars, and frees space for course content. An online syllabus with email reminders helps keep your students on schedule.

Sometimes, reducing the effort the students need to make in order to navigate through your course requires a great effort on your part. Anything you do to help your students navigate easily through your course, is worth the effort. The result is less time spent wondering what to do next, and more time spent on your course content.

10
Workshop Solution

Moodle's Workshop module is one of the most complex and powerful of all the activities. A workshop provides a place where the student can:

1. Receive directions for completing a project.
2. View an example of a completed project, provided by the teacher.
3. Assess the teacher's example using criteria given by the teacher.
4. Compare his/her assessment of the example to the teacher's assessment of the same example.
5. Submit his/her completed project.
6. Assess other students' completed projects, again using the criteria given by the teacher.
7. Compare his/her assessment of other students' work to the assessments made by other students, and by the teacher.
8. Receive assessments of the project that (s)he submitted.

I listed the workshop tasks in the order of which students usually complete them. You can skip some of these steps. However, the steps that can be skipped offer the most educational benefit.

For example, you can skip steps 3 and 4. If you do that, the workshop becomes a matter of just reading instructions on how to complete a project, viewing an example, and submitting the work. You might as well just use an Assignment instead. Assessing an example gives the student a clear idea about the teacher's expectations. By comparing his/her assessment to an assessment made by the teacher, confirms or denies the student's understanding of the expectations. This step is especially important if the student will be assessing other students' work.

Step 6 is also optional, but this can result in missed opportunities for learning. When a student is asked to assess another student's work, instead of just reading or reviewing it, the assessor is probably paying more attention to detail and spending more time on the work.

Steps 7 and 8 are also optional. As a teacher, you could just assess each student's work yourself. However, allowing a student to be assessed by others, and having him/her see how others assessed the work that (s)he assessed, makes the workshop a powerful collaborative experience.

This chapter will take you through the process of creating a full-featured workshop. It will not cover workshop administration, since Moodle's online documentation does an adequate job of explaining it. Instead, this chapter will focus on helping you to make decisions that create the kind of workshop experience you want your students to undergo.

Workshop Basics

Workshops are complex. There are a lot of moving parts, and most settings that you choose will affect or be affected by at least one other setting. Let us review some basic concepts before we talk about workshop specifics.

Plan your Strategy

When you create a Moodle workshop, you will enter several page's worth of information. But all the settings that you choose can be summarized into a few basic questions:

- What work do you want the student to submit?
- Will a student assess the work of his/her classmates, and if so, how will that affect the student's grade?
- How much of the student's grade depends on assessing the work of his/her peers, and how much of the work the student has submitted?
- What are the criteria for assessing the work?
- What submissions will the student assess— an example by the teacher, other students' work, and/or the student's own submission?
- If classmates assess each other's work, will they do this anonymously?
- Must the classmates agree on a grade, or can they make their assessments independent of each other?
- What is the schedule for submitting the work, and for submitting assessments?

Try to answer these questions before you begin creating your workshop. When you have answered them, you have created your workshop strategy. Then, as we step through creating a workshop, we will equate each setting with one of the questions.

Grading Grades

One of the most unique features of a workshop is that the student doesn't receive a grade only for the work that (s)he has submitted. The student can also receive a grade for the assessments that (s)he has performed. In other words, the student is graded on the grades that (s)he gives to others.

Step-by-Step Example: Create the Workshop

Let's begin our step-by-step example. We'll organize the steps using the questions from the section above.

What Work do you want the Student to Submit?

This is how you can get your students to submit their work:

1. From the **Add an activity** drop-down list, select **Workshop**. The **Editing Workshop** page is displayed.

2. Into the **Submission Title** field, enter the name of the workshop. Students will see this on the course home page.

3. When a student first enters the workshop, (s)he will see what you have entered in the **Description** field. This field can be both a description of the workshop, and instructions for completing the work. In the example below, you can see several features of a workshop description:

    ° The goal of the workshop. This is in the first sentence.

    ° An overview of what the student will do. This is in the second and third paragraphs.

    ° Step-by-step directions for completing the workshop. This example could be improved if the author included a link to a printer-friendly version of the instructions.

    ° A clear statement of what to do first. This is in the last sentence.

    ° The example is taken from an online photography course.

In this assignment, you will explore the limitations of your lens's depth of field.

You will take two pictures of a close-up subject. One picture will have a second subject in the medium background, six to eight feet from the lens. The other picture will have a second subject in the far background, over thirty feet from the lens. You will see the limitations on your lens's ability to simultaneously focus on a close-up subject and background subject.

Before taking and submitting your pictures, you must review the two examples provided by the instructor. Click the Assess link below to display the assessment form, and the links to the examples. Your submissions will be graded by the teacher, using the same form.

To complete this assignment:

Assess the two examples provided by the teacher.

Take the first photo. Place the main subject no more than three feet from the lens and a second subject six to eight feet from the lens. Name this picture yourname_close-med.jpg, where your name is your username.

Take the second photo. Place the main subject no more than three feet from the lens, and a second subject thirty or more feet from the lens. Name this picture yourname_close-far.jpg, where yourname is your username.

Attach the two photos. Below you see a form titled Submit your Assignment using this Form:, and below that you should see fields for Attachment 1: and Attachment 2:. Use those fields to attach your photos.

In the Title: field for the submission form, enter your username.

In the Description: field, for each picture, give the:

Distance from lens to closest subject.

Distance from lens to background subject.

Lens opening used.

Focal length used.

Finally, submit the assignment.

Begin now with Step 1, by clicking on the Assess link below.

In this example, the author gives complete instructions for completing the workshop. You might choose to enter a minimal description, and put the instructions in a web page or .pdf file instead.

Will a Student Assess the Work of his/her Classmates, and if so, How will that Affect the Student's Grade?

For the field **Grade for Assessments**, select a value. This value is the maximum grade the student can earn for assessing the work of his/her peers, and for assessing his/her own work.

This is not a grade for the work the student submitted. This is a grade for the assessments the student completed.

The teacher does not assign this grade. Instead, Moodle automatically calculates this grade. The calculation happens in one of two ways. If the teacher assesses a submission, Moodle compares the student's assessment of that submission with the teacher's. The closer the student comes to matching the teacher's assessment, the higher the student's **Grade for Assessment**. For example, if both Student 1 and the Teacher assessed the work of Student 2, and Student 1's assessment matched the Teacher's assessment almost exactly, then Student 1 would receive a high grade for that assessment.

Or, in case the teacher did not assess a submission, the student's assessment of that submission is compared with the assessments made by the other students in the class. The closer the assessment of the student is to the average, the better is the student's grade for that assessment. If a submission is assessed by one or two students, then that student(s) receives the best grade possible for their assessments. If a submission is assessed by three or more students, then the student's grade is closer to the average. Further down the page, you will choose the **Number of Assessments of Student Submissions**. This will determine how many submissions each student will assess. If you choose to have each student assess only 1 or 2 submissions, and the teacher is not assessing submissions, then expect them to score the maximum on the grade for assessments. This is not always bad. If you just want the student to have credit for trying the assessment, regardless of how well the student's assessment agrees with others, then this is a good option.

If you want the student to be graded on how close his/her assessment is to those of his/her peers, then the teacher should not perform any assessments, and you should have the student assess three or more submissions. If you want the student to be graded on how close his/her assessment is to that of the teacher's, then of course the teacher will need to assess each submission.

How much of the Student's Grade Depends on Assessing the Work of his/her Peers, and How much on the Work the Student has Submitted?

For the field **Grade for Submission**, select a value. This value is the maximum grade the student can earn for the work that (s)he submits.

The grade for submission is determined by the assessments that the teacher and/or classmates made of the work. If the student's work is assessed by only the teacher, then the grade for submission is whatever the teacher determines. If the student's work is assessed by his/her classmates, then the grade for submission is determined by their assessments. If both the teacher and classmates assessed the work, then the grade is affected by both.

Further down the page, you will choose the **Weight for Teacher Assessments**. This will determine how much weight the teacher's assessment of the work will have, compared to the peer assessments.

What is the Criteria for Assessing the Work?

Select a **Grading Strategy**. It determines how the student's work will be assessed by his/her classmates. Earlier on the **Editing Workshop** page, you selected the maximum **Grade for Submission**. When a student's submission is being assessed, the student is getting a grade for the submission. All of the assessments for a submission will be averaged and the grade for the submission will be calculated. More on how the grade is calculated is discussed later.

The online help gives complete explanations for each grading strategy. In brief, your choices are:

- **No grading**: When a classmate assesses the student's work, (s)he leaves comments but does not grade them. Recall that previously, we said the **Grade for Assessments** is calculated based on the scores a classmate gives when performing an assessment. If you select **No grading**, then a classmate is not giving any scores when he performs an assessment. The result is that Moodle cannot calculate a **Grade for Assessments** when the **Grading Strategy** is set to **No grading**. This would seem to put us in a quandary. If we base a part of each student's grade on the assessments that (s)he performs, but the assessments consist only of comments which Moodle cannot use to calculate a grade, how do we get a grade for the assessments? In this case, the teacher can grade the student's assessments. The maximum points that the teacher can give for this grade is set in the **Grade for Assessments**.

- **Accumulative grading**: In this strategy, the teacher creates several assessment elements. Each element is a specific, well-defined criterion for judging the work. And, each element can have its own grading scale. For example, here is an assessment element from a photography workshop. Note that in the following screenshot it uses a 2-point scale, and has a grade weight of 1 point:

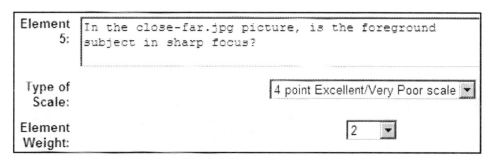

Here is another assessment element from the same workshop. Note that this one uses a 4-point scale, and has a grade weight of 2 points:

Element 5:	In the close-far.jpg picture, is the foreground subject in sharp focus?
Type of Scale:	4 point Excellent/Very Poor scale ▼
Element Weight:	2 ▼

- **Error Banded Grading**: The submission is assessed using a set of Yes/No criteria. Using **Error Banded Grading**, an assessment element would look like this:

Element 1:	Does the closeup subject appear to be within three feet of the lens?
Element Weight:	1 ▼

Note the default **Element Weight** is **1**

The grade is determined by a **Grade Table**, which lists the grade the student earns when a given number of assessment elements are negative. This is shown in the following screenshot:

Grade Table	
Number of Negative Responses	Suggested Grade
0	10 ▾
1	9 ▾
2	7 ▾
3	6 ▾
4	4 ▾
5	3 ▾
6	1 ▾
7	0 ▾
8	0 ▾
9	0 ▾

- **Criterion**: With a Criterion strategy, the assessor just chooses a grade, and adjustment, and optionally leaves comments. This is shown in the following screenshot:

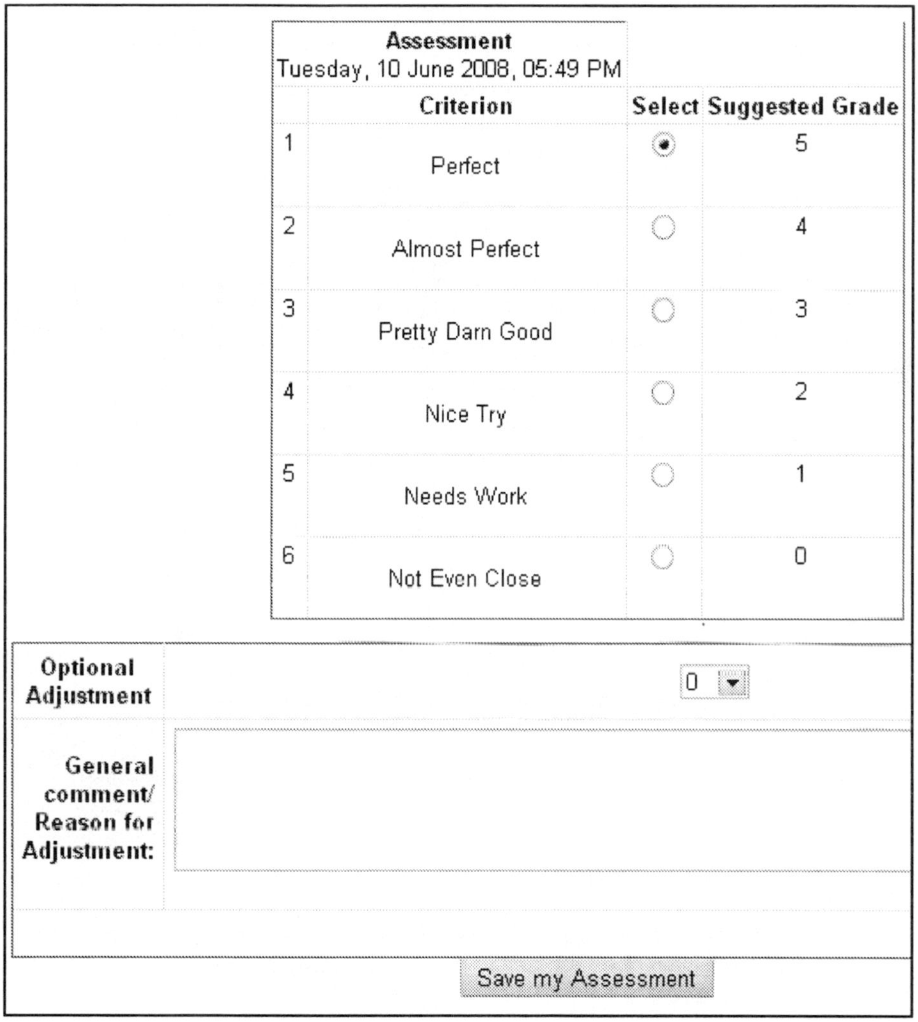

	Criterion	Select	Suggested Grade
	Assessment Tuesday, 10 June 2008, 05:49 PM		
1	Perfect	●	5
2	Almost Perfect	○	4
3	Pretty Darn Good	○	3
4	Nice Try	○	2
5	Needs Work	○	1
6	Not Even Close	○	0

Optional Adjustment	0 ▼
General comment/ Reason for Adjustment:	

Save my Assessment

- **Rubric**: The Rubric assessment strategy is like Criterion, but instead of giving one overall rating for the entire submission, you choose one rating for each aspect of the submission. In this example, the student assesses a photograph on its focus and lighting:

Assessment
Wednesday, 31 December 1969, 07:00 PM
The Grade is : 0.00 (Maximum grade 10)

Element 1:   Focus

Weight: 2.00

Select   **Criterion**

   ⊙   All elements of the picture are out of focus.

   ○   Only the least important elements of the picture are in focus.

   ○   Only the most important elements of the picture are in focus.

   ○   All elements of the picture are in focus.

Feedback: Your Feedback goes Here

Element 2:   Lighting

Weight: 1.00

Select   **Criterion**

   ⊙   All elements of the picture are either too dark to see detail, or too washed out to see proper color.

   ○   Some elements of the picture are either too dark to see detail, or too washed out to see proper color.

   ○   All elements of the picture are properly lit.

Select a value for **Number of Comments, Assessment Elements, Grade Bands, Criterion Statements,** or **Categories in a Rubric**.

- **Number of Comments** applies if you chose a **Grading Strategy— Not Graded**. Remember that with this grading strategy, the assessor doesn't give a grade, but instead only leaves comments.
- **Assessment Elements** applies if you chose **Accumulative grading**.
- **Grade Bands** applies if you chose **Error Banded Grading**.
- **Criterion Statements** applies if you chose **Criterion**.
- **Categories in a** Rubric applies if you chose **Rubric**.

Select the **Number of Attachments expected on Submissions**. This does not set the minimum or maximum number of attachments that a student can upload. Instead, it just creates a given number of upload boxes. See the online help for more explanation.

Choose if you will **Allow Resubmissions**. Recall that previously, you chose a **Grade for Submission**. If you allow resubmissions, the student's **Grade for Submission** will be that of the submission with the highest grade.

What Submissions will the Student Assess?

A student can assess—an example by the teacher, other students' work, and/or the student's own submission.

If the setting **Number of Assessments of Examples from Teacher**, is set to number other than **0**, the student must assess examples provided by the teacher before (s)he can upload a submission.

Select a value for **Comparison of Assessments**. Remember that previously you chose a **Grade for Assessments**. Recall that if the teacher assesses the submissions, then a student's grade for assessments is calculated by comparing it to the teacher's assessments. If the teacher does not assess the submissions, then a student's grade for assessments is calculated by comparing it to the assessments made by the rest of the class. This setting determines how closely the student's assessment must agree with the teacher's, or with the class average, for a submission. For example, if this is set to **Very Lax**, and there are 10 yes/no assessment criteria, an assessment that agrees with the teacher on 8 of the 10 criteria would earn a grade of 80%. But if it is set to **Very Strict**, it would earn a grade of 35%.

The setting **Number of Assessments of Student Submissions** determines how many submissions each student will be asked to assess. If this is set to zero, then students do not assess each other's work.

Recall that the grade is calculated from the assessments made of that submission. The **Weight for Teacher Assessments** determines how much the Teacher's assessment affects that grade. You select how many student assessments the Teacher's assessment is worth. If this is set to **0**, the teacher's assessment is not used when determining a student's grade for submissions.

As students submit or upload their work to a workshop, Moodle allocates it to other students for assessment. The field **Number of Assessments of Student Submissions** determines how many submissions each student is required to assess. Ideally, everyone will submit their assignments on time, and the students will have plenty of time to evaluate each other's work. For example, suppose there are 10 students in the class, and **Number of Assessments of Student Submissions** is set to **3**. That means, each of the ten submissions is assessed three times. Moodle assigns the assessments as the work is submitted.

However, if a student submits work late, the students who are going to evaluate the late person's work will need to wait before they can complete their assessments. Let us suppose one student doesn't submit his/her work by the deadline. That means the class is three assessments short. Since Moodle assigns the assessments evenly, three students will end the class one assessment short. Shall we penalize these students for not completing the required three assessments?

In our example, **Over Allocation** is set to **0**, and each submission is evaluated three and only three times. If we set **Over Allocation** to **1**, then when the deadline arrives, Moodle will over allocate some work to the students who still need to complete their assessments. In this example, Moodle will randomly choose three pieces of work that have already been assessed three times, and assign them to the three students who are missing an assessment. These pieces of work will then be over allocated by one assessment each. Moodle allows a maximum over allocation of two.

If **Self Assessment** is set to **Yes**, each student is asked to evaluate his or her own work. This is in addition to the number of student submissions that the student is asked to evaluate.

If Classmates Assess Each Others' Work, will They do it Anonymously?

If **Assessments must be agreed** is set to **Yes**, then an assessment made by one student can be viewed by the other reviewers of the same work. If the other reviewers disagree, the evaluation process continues until they agree or until the assignment's closing time is passed. This can be a useful tool for determining how clear your evaluation elements are. If there is a lot of disagreement among reviewers of the same work, revisit your evaluation elements and the instructions you gave the reviewers.

Must the Classmates Agree on a Grade, or Can they Make their Assessments Independent of Each Other?

The **Hide Grades Before Agreement** setting, affects the assessment process only if **Assessments must be agreed** is set to **Yes**. If **Hide Grades Before Agreement** is set to **Yes**, the numeric parts of a project's evaluation are hidden from other reviewers. The reviewers can see each other's comments, but not the grades they've assigned. The grades will appear after the reviewers have chosen the same grade, or the closing time has passed.

The **League Table of Submitted Work** setting creates a list of the best-rated assignments in this workshop. If set to zero, no list is created.

If **Hide Names from Students** is set to **Yes**, evaluators are given the name of the person whose work they are assessing. Note that the names of students are never hidden from the teacher. Also, if a teacher assesses a student's work, the teacher cannot do so anonymously. This only hides the names of students who submitted work from the students who are evaluating the work.

The **Use Password** and **Password** fields can be used to protect the assessment. Note that all students have the same password.

Maximum Size sets the size limit for project files uploaded to the workshop. This cannot be greater than the limit set for the site.

What is the Schedule for Submitting the Work, and Assessments?

The fields for **Start and End of Submissions/Assessments** determine when the workshop opens and closes. On the closing date, students can no longer upload files, or evaluate others' work. If any grades are hidden, they appear.

You can start the assessments before the end of the submissions. This will give students more time to assess their classmates' work. You can also have a delay between the end of submissions and the beginning of assessments. This gives you time to examine the submissions before having the class assess them. You can determine if the work is close to what you expected or were trying to elicit from the students. You might even want to use the time between submission and assessment to refine your assessment criteria, in response to the work submitted.

Summary

The key to a Workshop is not what kind of work you will have the student submit, but your assessment strategy. An assessment strategy determines what the students assess, how they assess the work, if they must agree on their assessments, if their assessments must agree with yours, and how much of their grade depends upon completing assessments.

If the work that the student produces is the most important part, you may as well use a simple Assignment instead. It is the assessment strategy that makes a Workshop different form the other modules.

Index

P

pre-correction
  about 14
  uses 15
previous chats, chat uses
  about 52
  including 52-54
  transcript, copying 52, 53
principles and activities
  about 10
  big ideas 11
  distributed practice 11
  guided notes 12
  immediate error correction 12
  juxtapose 13
  lesson outline 14
  mnemonics 14
  Moodle features, mapped to 18
  pre-correction 14
  response cards 15
  self monitoring 16
  Socratic dialogue 17
  time trials 17
proctored quiz
  full IP addresses 77
  hosting, from secured location 77
  IP addresses, determining 81, 82
  netwotk address types 77-79
  partial IP addresses 79

Q

quizzes
  about 63
  distributed practice 63
  feedback, adding to questions 70-75
  feedback, for multiple choice question 70, 71
  feedback, for multiple numeric question 73, 74
  making 69
  proctored quiz 77
  self assessment, excluding from Gradebook 67
  self assessment, using for 66-69
  specific questions, need for 69
  timed quizzes 75

R

response cards
  about 15
  versus quiz 16
reviewing papers, chat uses
  about 49
  one-on-one chat 49
  one-on-one chat, chat hiding 50, 51
  one-on-one chat, groups using 50

S

self monitoring 16
sequential activities
  activity locking 88
  need for 88
  versus activity locking 88
single-student forum
  creating 22
  creating for group 22
  creating for student 22
  group, creating for each student 27-29
  students, enrolling 25-27
single-student wiki
  about 109
  creating 109
  guided note, taking 110
  guided notes, leveraging 119
  individual student wiki, creating 116
  links to other starting pages, creating 114
  multiple starting pages, creating 112-114
  multiple text files, for multiple starting pages 114
  testing as student 117, 118
  text file creating, for starting page 110-112
  text file uploading, for starting page 115, 116
  text filex selecting, for initial pages 117
Socratic dialogue 17
split discussions
  about 38
  change of meaning 38-40
  replies, moving 41

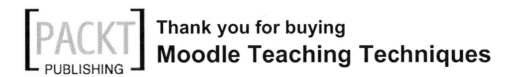

Thank you for buying
Moodle Teaching Techniques

Packt Open Source Project Royalties

When we sell a book written on an Open Source project, we pay a royalty directly to that project. Therefore by purchasing Moodle Teaching Techniques, Packt will have given some of the money received to the Moodle Project.

In the long term, we see ourselves and you — customers and readers of our books — as part of the Open Source ecosystem, providing sustainable revenue for the projects we publish on. Our aim at Packt is to establish publishing royalties as an essential part of the service and support a business model that sustains Open Source.

If you're working with an Open Source project that you would like us to publish on, and subsequently pay royalties to, please get in touch with us.

Writing for Packt

We welcome all inquiries from people who are interested in authoring. Book proposals should be sent to authors@packtpub.com. If your book idea is still at an early stage and you would like to discuss it first before writing a formal book proposal, contact us; one of our commissioning editors will get in touch with you.

We're not just looking for published authors; if you have strong technical skills but no writing experience, our experienced editors can help you develop a writing career, or simply get some additional reward for your expertise.

About Packt Publishing

Packt, pronounced 'packed', published its first book "Mastering phpMyAdmin for Effective MySQL Management" in April 2004 and subsequently continued to specialize in publishing highly focused books on specific technologies and solutions.

Our books and publications share the experiences of your fellow IT professionals in adapting and customizing today's systems, applications, and frameworks. Our solution-based books give you the knowledge and power to customize the software and technologies you're using to get the job done. Packt books are more specific and less general than the IT books you have seen in the past. Our unique business model allows us to bring you more focused information, giving you more of what you need to know, and less of what you don't.

Packt is a modern, yet unique publishing company, which focuses on producing quality, cutting-edge books for communities of developers, administrators, and newbies alike. For more information, please visit our website: www.PacktPub.com.

Moodle E-Learning Course Development

ISBN: 1-904811-29-9   Paperback: 250 pages

A complete guide to successful learning
using Moodle

1. Straight-forward coverage of installing and
    using the Moodle system

2. Working with Moodle features in all learning
    environments

3. A unique course-based approach focuses
    your attention on designing well structured,
    interactive, and successful courses

Building Websites with Joomla!
1.5 Beta 1

ISBN: 978-1-847192-38-7   Paperback: 380 pages

The bestselling Joomla tutorial guide updated for the
latest download release

1. Install and configure Joomla! 1.5 beta 1

2. Customize and extend your Joomla! site

3. Create your own template and extensions

4. **Free eBook upgrades up to 1.5 Final Release**

5. Also available covering Joomla v1

Please check **www.PacktPub.com** for information on our titles

PUBLISHING

Drupal

ISBN: 1-904811-80-9   Paperback: 267 pages

How to setup, configure and customise this powerful PHP/MySQL based Open Source CMS

1. Install, configure, administer, maintain and extend Drupal

2. Control access with users, roles and permissions

3. Structure your content using Drupal's powerful CMS features

4. Includes coverage of release 4.7

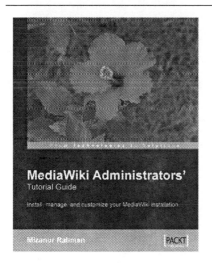

MediaWiki Administrators' Tutorial Guide

ISBN: 978-1-904811-59-6   Paperback: 284 pages

Install, manage, and customize your MediaWiki installation

1. Get your MediaWiki site up fast

2. Manage users, special pages, and more

3. Customize and extend your MediaWiki site

4. Create new, attractive MediaWiki themes

Please check **www.PacktPub.com** for information on our titles

Printed in the United Kingdom by
Lightning Source UK Ltd., Milton Keynes
140394UK00001B/53/A

9 781847 192844